Regaining Your Spiritual Poise

How Christians Can Regain Balance and
Meaning in Their Lives through the Practice
of Retreat and Christian Spirituality

ROB WINGERTER

WESTBOW
PRESS
A DIVISION OF THOMAS NELSON

WestBow Press books may be ordered through booksellers or by contacting:

WestBow Press
A Division of Thomas Nelson
1663 Liberty Drive
Bloomington, IN 47403
www.westbowpress.com
1 (866) 928-1240

Because of the dynamic nature of the Internet, any web addresses or links contained in
this book may have changed since publication and may no longer be valid. The views
expressed in this work are solely those of the author and do not necessarily reflect the
views of the publisher, and the publisher hereby disclaims any responsibility for them.

Unless otherwise noted, scripture quotations are from The Holy Bible,
English Standard Version® (ESV®), copyright © 2001 by Crossway, a publishing
ministry of Good News Publishers. Used by permission. All rights reserved.

ISBN: 978-1-4908-2079-8 (sc)
ISBN: 978-1-4908-2080-4 (hc)
ISBN: 978-1-4908-2078-1 (e)

Library of Congress Control Number: 2013923149

Printed in the United States of America.

WestBow Press rev. date: 1/9/2014

Contents

Preface

Mark Twain once observed, "A classic is a book everyone wants to have read, but no one wants to read one." I think there is a corollary in the Christian life. Everyone wants to have led a dynamic, sold-out, impactful Christian life—but no one wants to lead one. Most Christians have a conversion experience that starts off their Christian lives with a great deal of energy and focus. Much like a rocket ship, they blast off with great vigor and enthusiasm in their newfound faith. However, just as the gravitational field of the earth pulls the rocket ship back toward the launch pad, the Christian is pulled back to unbelief (or at least toward lethargy) by the cares of this world. Sin, boredom, cultural attractions, doubt, and fear all rob the Christian of the energy needed to lead the Christ-centered life God planned for His people.

I won't pretend that this one small book written by a layman will provide all of the insights necessary to inspire every professing Christian to become a spiritual giant. However, I do hope in some small way that some of the observations contained herein will be helpful in moving Christ seekers just a little further down the path of spiritual maturity. My primary focus will be on recapturing an all but forgotten practice of personal retreat. In particular among the American Protestant community, the concept of taking time out of one's "busy schedule" to spend time in isolation for the purpose of prayer and contemplation seems archaic and unappealing. Even among those churches that have men's or women's "retreats," these retreats almost invariably take the form of corporate seminars with guest speakers who often give self-help messages. This lack of understanding of true retreat robs the average Christian of the energy source necessary to sustain one through life's spiritual ups and downs.

By background and training, I am a certified public accountant and an attorney. To say that I am left-brain dominant would be an understatement. As such, when addressing the subject of retreat, I won't be approaching the idea from a touchy-feely perspective. To thine own self be true. Rather, I have tried to lay out the idea of retreat from an historical and practical perspective. Under the general theory of informing people by telling them what you are going to tell them, then telling them, and then telling them what you told them, I have approached the topic of retreat using the following approach.

Chapter one will lay the groundwork for why retreat is so necessary in our lives. One of the most succinct summations of the need for retreat in our lives comes from the English Christian mystic Evelyn Underhill. She stated,

> We come [in to retreat] to seek the opportunity of being alone with God and attending to God in order that we may do his will better in our ordinary lives. We come to live for a few days the life of prayer and deepen our contact with the spiritual realities on which our lives depend—to recover if we can our spiritual poise. We do not come for spiritual information, but for spiritual food and air—to wait on the Lord and renew our strength—not for our own sake but for the sake of the world.[1]

If spiritual retreat is so necessary, then why is it so lacking in the Christian world today? That will be the focus of chapter two of the book. Notice that I focus on its absence in Protestant world today. That is not to say that retreat as a spiritual practice is totally lacking in the Christian world. A quick search of Christian retreat centers on the Internet will list hundreds of retreat centers in the United States. However, a cursory review will tell you that the vast majority of those listed (in excess of 80 percent) have a connection to or were founded by one of the Roman Catholic holy orders. Chapter two will explore this phenomenon as well.

Chapters three and four will explore the monastic movement. Beginning with the early desert fathers of the fourth century through the later monastic movements of the Middle Ages, we will examine the call to live lives with a singular focus on spiritual connectivity to our Lord and Savior. A cursory observation may be that the monastic movement would have little applicability in the modern Christian's life. My goal is to demonstrate that the calling of these early monks and sisters in reality is the same call we are answering in our own limited way when we enter in to retreat.

Chapter five will explore the topic of Christian spirituality. In particular it will examine the lives of select men and women who exhibited a life of focused intensity of the triune God.

In chapter six there will be a short overview of those classic spiritual disciplines most appropriate to practice in a retreat setting. This does not mean that these disciplines can't be practiced outside of retreat. However, without some insights into the activities to be undertaken when someone makes the time in his or her schedule to "get away," there is always the potential that a spiritual retreat will just turn in to a weekend away.

For too many western Christians, the idea of practicing the spiritual disciplines in a retreat scenario may have the negative connotation of Eastern mysticism and feel taboo. The reality of the matter is that Christian mysticism or spirituality has a deep history in the Christian tradition. Unlike Eastern religious mysticism, which is often designed to empty your mind (and thus let anything in), Christian meditative practices are designed to bring singular focus on our God and Savior.

At this point, most discerning Christians should ask the legitimate question: "This all sounds good, but what does the Bible have to say about the idea of retreat?" The short answer is "A lot." Jesus Christ himself set the pattern for retreat and that will be the subject of chapter seven of the book.

Now, presuming I have you convinced that you want to make spiritual retreats a part of your life, chapter eight will address the question of "How do I get started?" Chapters nine and ten will address the practical side of the structure and potential content of your retreat.

Although this book was written to extol the benefits of retreat, the real goal is to encourage individual to keep the spirit of retreat alive throughout the year. Chapter eleven will address this topic.

Finally, in chapter twelve, I will discuss some personal history and why I felt compelled to write this book. I will review the story of Mahseh, the Christian retreat center that I helped found and now work at. The lessons learned over the last seven years form the basis for most of the content of this book. The story of Mahseh is one that confirms to me of God's desire to act directly in each believer's life to see that individuals grow and mature in their faith.

My sincere hope for all who read this book is that it be half as edifying for them as it was for me to write it. I also trust that the experience of spiritual retreat will allow readers to grow in their own personal walks of faith and thereby enhance their lives and the lives of those around them.

Rob Wingerter
October 2013

Chapter 1: Retreat—Who Needs It?

Think back to your moment of conversion. If you are like most people, there was an initial period of exhilaration that came with the realization that you were now a child of God. There was a feeling of relief of guilt, spiritual renewal, and love for our Savior that was both humbling and invigorating. Believers have a sense of joy (to borrow a phrase from C. S. Lewis) in their lives. Many of us determine to lead lives indicative of our new relationship. We increase or begin our church attendance, participate in more Bible studies, pray with more fervency, and attempt to lead lives that honor God.

But then what happens? Slowly, old habits return. Church attendance becomes less regular (or less meaningful). Time in prayer and study of the Word begins to wane. We more frequently catch ourselves operating with a worldly mind-set instead of leading lives that have an eternal perspective guiding them. Just like a rocket ship that blasts off with great energy and power, the inevitable pull of gravity brings us back toward practical unbelief. Is this just the way it is? After all, we are just human.

If we look to some of the root causes of this gravitational pull toward unbelief we will be better equipped to counteract this force. It will also be more evident how the practice of retreat can be a critical element toward recovering this lost joy of our initial launch into our Christian faith.

Root Causes: Sin

Undoubtedly the core issue that impacts our ability to lead lives as committed Christians is the fact that we are still fallen creatures, and as such, sin is still prevalent in our lives. This sinful condition is not just a problem for the spiritually immature. Take a look at what Paul had to say about sin in his life in Romans 7:14–23.

> For we know that the law is spiritual, but I am of the flesh, sold under sin. For I do not understand my own actions. For I do not do what I want, but I do the very thing I hate. Now if I do what I do not want, I agree with the law and that is good. So now it is no longer I who do it, but sin that dwells within me. For I know that nothing good dwells in me, that is, in my flesh. For I have the desire to do what is right, but not the ability to carry it out. For I do not do the good that I want, but the evil I do not want is what I keep on doing. Now if I do what I do not want, it is no longer I who do it, but sin that dwells within me.

Remember who is saying this. This is Paul the apostle—Saint Paul, the writer of half of the New Testament. This would be pretty discouraging if the end of the story was just to live with sin in our lives. A pattern of sin in our lives hardens our hearts.[2] When our hearts are hardened, we do not allow ourselves to be open to the leadings of the Holy Spirit and the guidance of wise counsel. We become inwardly focused and attempt to become self-sufficient. We begin to distance ourselves from the Lord, and even though He never abandons us, we attempt to abandon or ignore Him. When this happens, it is easy to feel distant and uninspired.

Worse yet, sin is very habit-forming. When we first relent and fall prey to sin, it may singe our conscience. However, each time we commit the same sin afterward, it becomes easier. Pretty soon we make excuses and eventually even play God and do not even call our actions sin. As Paul said above, what wicked men and women we are!

What is the answer? How can we avoid sin? We get some guidance from 1 John 1:8–9.

> If we say we have no sin, we deceive ourselves and the truth is not in us. If we confess our sins, he is faithful and just to forgive us our sins and to cleanse us from all unrighteousness.

Confession of our sins and prayer to guard us against future sin seems to be the key to minimizing the impact of sin in our lives. Confession requires communication, communication creates relationships, and relationships create an increasing bond that will make us more Christlike. This allows us to live lives more closely aligned with what the Father has in store for His children.

If communication and prayer are keys to a renewed life, we need to create space in our lives to have time to practice these disciplines. As will be discussed later in this book, the habit of retreat builds this space in our lives to allow for a focused time of confession and prayer.

Root Causes: The Pull of Culture

As if sin in our lives was not enough, there are several other factors that retard our spiritual growth. Next, let us explore the impact of culture on our growth into spiritual maturity.

Francis Schaeffer did a masterful job of outlining the separation of the spiritual from everyday life in his early works *Escape from Reason*[3] and *The God Who Is There*[4]. Although certainly not an exhaustive analysis of all the events that resulted in our current bifurcated approach to life, his analysis does provide a reasoned basis for explaining the pervasive attitude among many Christians and non-Christians that church is a Sunday morning activity.

Summarizing his key thoughts, the combination of scientific analysis and philosophical thought led to a separation of spiritual matters from the nonspiritual. Utilizing Schaeffer's classic analogy, mankind established an upper and lower story for purposes of warehousing everyday actions and thoughts. If something was provable under scientific analysis, it was placed in the lower story. If not, it resided in the upper story.

Schaeffer then argued that the introduction of Georg Hegel's dialectic[5] opened the door for the proposition of the "loss of absolutes." Hegel is most noted for the concept that each proposition or thesis can be opposed with an antithesis. After a period of time, a dialogue between proponents of each results in a synthesis, or new thought. Since this process can be repeated an indefinite number of times, there is a constant refinement and redefinition of any proposition. Other than scientific facts that are fixed by the laws of nature, any nonscientific proposition is subject to future refinement.

Applied back to the upper and lower story, those ideas (such as religious faith) that reside in the upper story really have the status of opinions rather than facts. As such, they are subject to this process of continuous redefinition. With this cultural framework, the modern Christian is faced with the dilemma that his faith in Christ is really just his opinion. If he gains comfort from such beliefs, that is fine for him. However, one's faith is an entirely personal matter and best practiced in private on a Sunday morning with other individuals who just happen to "feel" the same way he does.

The purpose of this book is not to explain why this attitude toward faith is wrong. There are numerous volumes of apologetics that can respond to this issue. Suffice it to say that our Christian faith is a well-reasoned faith. Certainly within the definitions of legal proof, the historic existence and resurrection of Jesus can be proven. In addition, the reliability of the Bible as God's written Word to us can be reasonably accepted by an individual who has an open mind on the subject.

This pull of culture toward unbelief can be overwhelming and has only become more so with the advancement of technology that is now pervasive in our lives. The onslaught of information and ideas can leave one bewildered. Anyone with access to the Internet can locate volumes of information on any topic regardless of the quality of correctness of the ideas expressed.

We would all like to think that we can overcome this spiritual malaise imposed by the culture around us by just ignoring it. However, this book proposes that only by temporarily extracting oneself from the everyday activities and surroundings can you give yourself a real opportunity to reground yourself in the reasons for your faith and prepare yourself to go forth on your daily journey. By isolating yourself, even for only a few days a year, from the activities, concerns, pressures, and demands of daily living, you can truly regain your spiritual poise.

Even the act itself of making time in your schedule for an overnight retreat is countercultural. We live in a society that places demands on us 24/7. The thought of making time in our hectic schedules to get away and just spend time in prayer, meditation, and study just doesn't sound very practical. However, once you try it you can see what a life-affirming event it can be.

Root Causes: Boredom

The prayer of Agur in Proverbs 30:8–9 is one of the more unusual prayers in the Bible.

> Remove far from me vanity and lies: give me neither poverty nor riches; feed me with the food convenient for me. Lest I be full, and deny thee, and say "Who is the Lord?" or lest I be poor, and steal, and take the name of my God in vain.[6]

One of the most prayed prayers in the world is the Lord's Prayer, the Our Father. We pray to God the Father to "give us our daily bread." How many of you have heard someone add the admonition "and Father, please don't make me rich"? That just is not in our nature. We always seem to want more. Yet Agur recognized one of the flaws we have in our nature. If we are too comfortable, we often forget the Lord and become lackadaisical in our faith.

Agur's prayer was basically "Don't let me be too comfortable." That's against human nature. We want to stay in our comfort zone, where it's warm, comfortable, and secure. Just as a bird feathers its nest, we want things to be soft, insulated, and familiar, but when you fail to break out of your comfort zone, boredom results—and boredom kills.

Look to John 15: 5: "I am the vine, you are the branches; apart from me nothing can be accomplished. He who abides in me bears much fruit." You can only accomplish something of spiritual significance if you depend on Christ. But you need to break out of your comfort zone in order to rely on Christ. When you are in water over your head, you will need Him. When you are just standing on the pier, you don't need Him, and He doesn't use you.

John Trapp wrote, "He that cannot pray, let him go to sea and there he will learn." If you say you can't pray—maybe you have never put yourself into a situation where you needed to pray. Lack of prayer life may just be an indication that you haven't left your comfort zone and don't feel the need to pray. But isn't this abandoning your comfort zone scary? Yes, but it is biblical.

Think back to Exodus and the story of Moses. Egyptians had enslaved the Israelites. They were being persecuted mercilessly. Someone needed to do something about it, and Moses would appear to be the ideal person. At age forty, he was in the prime of life. He was a Hebrew by birth but was raised in the royal court. He sensed he was the perfect person to correct things. Then one day, a fight broke out between an Egyptian and a Hebrew, and Moses solved the problem by killing the Egyptian. Killing Egyptians one at a time was a slow solution to the problem. God then sent him into the wilderness for forty years. When God came to him again and asked him to return to Egypt, he was eighty years of age. He said he was too old and slow of speech and couldn't accomplish the task. At that point God told him that he was ready.[7]

Hopefully not many of us will need a forty-year retreat to soften our hearts to do what God has planned for us. However, unless we break out of our comfort zones and confront God in a personal and intimate way, we may never truly feel His calling.

There is an old story attributed to Martin Luther. It is the story of the demon's reporting on their mischief back to Satan. The first team reports that they found a band of Christians crossing the desert and caused a sandstorm to come up and kill them all. Satan says, "Not bad, but they were Christians, and now they are just at home with the Lord." The second demon states that he found a shipload of Christians crossing the ocean and caused a great typhoon to come up, and now they are at the bottom of the sea. Again, Satan says, "Not bad, but again, you just sent them home to be with the Lord." The third demon gets up and says, "I have spent the last ten years lulling one Christian to sleep, and I just left him in his church," and all of the demons and Satan, upon hearing this, danced for joy. The moral of the story: boredom kills, and it is contagious.

The opportunity to spend time in retreat on a regular basis provides this opportunity to get out of our comfort zones. We are breaking our normal, daily routine. We are removing the distractions that can keep us from establishing true community with our God. We can challenge ourselves to step out in faith in our lives and to put ourselves in situations that require us to be more reliant on the Lord. It may be uncomfortable at first, but as we mature, we will realize that we are growing in our faith, and our ability to make a difference in this world will make us wonder why we always wanted to play it safe.

Root Causes: An Entertainment Culture

Related to the root cause of boredom is the secondary problem of living in a culture of entertainment. In Neil Postman's 1985 book *Amusing Ourselves to Death*[8] he warns us that although many Americans feared the totalitarian state that was exemplified in George Orwell's *Nineteen Eighty-Four*, where minds were controlled by brute force; the real threat to our society is better captured by Aldous Huxley *Brave New World*, where our actions are controlled by our addiction to amusement.

Postman goes on to explain that particularly with the dawn of television, our perception of the world has been altered. Even the news has become a commodity that is packaged in such a way that it fits neatly in to the shortened episodic integrated with commercials. This is quickly followed by the latest mind-numbing situational comedy or reality show. When we have events spoon-fed to us in such a visual way, the desire and pretty soon the skill to independently analyze, research, and conclude on the activities of the day is atrophied. Television alone is not the only culprit. Think of how advertising has influenced our outlook on every aspect of life.

Several years ago I purchased an issue of *Time* dated September 8, 1947. I acquired the magazine because the cover featured C. S. Lewis. I wanted the opportunity to read about Lewis as his contemporaries viewed him. This was pre-Chronicles of Narnia, and Lewis had made a name for himself as a Christian apologist, primarily due to his BBC radio broadcasts that were to serve as the foundation for his book *Mere Christianity*. What struck me as particularly remarkable were the length of the article and the complexity of the syntax and sentence structure. For a magazine designed for the reading pleasure of the general public, I viewed it as very challenging read.

The other thing that I noticed was how simple or maybe even simplistic the advertising was in the magazine. The advertisements were heavy on words and without exception in a rather nondramatic way outlined the utilitarian value of the product. Most of the pictures were actually unsophisticated drawings in lieu of highly professionalized photographs.

I then went to the local bookstore and purchased that current week's *Time*. There was very little in the way of in-depth articles in the magazine. Most of the topics warranted little more than a few hundred words, what some critics might call bathroom-reading-length writing. The content also seemed to have shifted from world and business news to entertainment news.

The change in the content and style of the advertising was remarkable. Word-intense advertising had given way to highly graphic and visual-oriented publishing. Even more remarkable was that the product being advertised was not always evident at first glance. Many of the pages featured athletes or other celebrities with one-word captions like "unstoppable" or "invincible," and only by a careful analysis of the advertisement could you find the watch or the clothing that evidently made the wearer "unstoppable" or "invincible." The advertisements had become more sophisticated and were selling based on image of the buyer instead of the quality and usefulness of the product.

In just the short span of sixty years between the two magazines, we had come full circle from where the articles were sophisticated and the advertising simplistic to where the reading material was simplistic and the advertising sophisticated. Is it little wonder that today's generation (or arguably the last couple of generations) have had the way they look at and analyze God's world and world events around them altered? Many people have lost the ability to think deeply or read richly.

A recent survey had the following startling statistics:[9]

> Eighty percent of families will not even buy one book in a given twelve-month period.
>
> Forty-two percent of college students will never read another book after graduating.
>
> Fifty percent of all Americans cannot read an eighth-grade-level book.

With this kind of degenerative state of thoughtful reflection and reading, is it any wonder that many Christians are losing the ability to reflect deeply on their faith and are relegating religion to just an emotional experience? Again, as this book progresses, the ability to separate oneself for even a few days to reanchor one's faith on the bedrock of prayer, contemplation, study, and meditation can prove invaluable to staving off this culture of mind-numbing entertainment.

Root Causes: Fear and Shame

The last of the root causes that will be explored is one that is particularly sinister and troubling: the issues of fear and shame regarding the open practice of one's faith. This is not the fear that someone might have that lives in a part of the world where physical persecution and even death for openly practicing the Christian faith might occur. Rather, this is the fear that is accompanied by the shame of having your earthly reputation among your peers and neighbors at stake because they do not share your convictions about Jesus Christ. This is not the healthy fear that is being addressed in Proverbs 14:26, when the Bible states, "In the fear of the Lord one has strong confidence and his children will have refuge." For this is not fear *of* the Lord, this is rather fear *of being associated with* the Lord. This is a fear that comes from being ashamed to be too visible about your faith.

Now, when you think about this situation, it is comical (in a tragic sort of way)! This is the Lord God Almighty—the maker of heaven and earth. He has the immutable characteristics of omnipotence, omniscience, and omnipresence. For us, His very finite creation, to be ashamed and afraid of being associated with him would be akin to us picking up an ant off the ground and having the ant say, "Could you put me down? I don't want my friends to see me hanging around with you."

You may laugh at the above scenario, but think honestly about your actions. It would be the rare individual who could unequivocally state that they had never hidden their faith from the public eye on occasion. Have you ever entered a restaurant with your Bible at the conclusion of a church service and "conveniently" covered it up with your coat? How about running in to an old friend as you exited a worship rally who asked you what you were doing only to hear your lips reply, "Nothing really." To make the matter even more relevant (and potentially more painful), how about the times you are with family and friends and the topic of faith comes up and you remain painfully silent instead of giving the reason for the faith that is in you? Have you heard the cock crow three times in your life as well?

Why aren't we the fearless, outspoken Christians we long to be? What are we afraid of? First, we fear of letting go of our reputations. Second, we have doubts about our faith. Lastly, we fear letting go of our piece of this world.

Woodrow Wilson once said, "I suspect it is as difficult doing your job with men sneering at you as it is shooting at you." We all have egos and feel the need for acceptance. However, the reality every Christian has to face is that if you want to be the most popular person by earthly standards in your group of acquaintances, you will find it very difficult to live a consistently God-directed life. Unless you isolate yourself from the world (which isn't the biblical perspective that asks us to be salt and light to the world[10]), you are going to find yourself in situations where you will either have to go along to get along or you will need to stand up for your Christian principles and risk being rejected. Our reputation, if measured by human standards, may in fact suffer for our faith. That should not be a surprise to any student of church history, as Christians have suffered down through the centuries for their unwillingness to compromise to the spirit of the age. As Paul encouraged us in 2 Timothy 1:8,

> Therefore do not be ashamed of the testimony about our God, nor of me his prisoner, but share in suffering for the gospel by the power of God who saved us and called us to a holy calling, not because of our works but because of his own purpose and grace, which he gave us Christ Jesus before the ages began.

We also have fear and shame because we often have doubts about our faith. Anyone who says they have never had any doubts or questions about their faith is either in denial or brain-dead. We are not yet sanctified creatures, and there are mysteries about our faith we will not understand this side of heaven. The worse thing we can do is to suppress these questions. This only deepens the fear and shame. Rather, we should confess our questions and then seek wisdom and guidance through study of the Scripture and the counsel of wise men. There is only one unanswered question contained in the word of God, and that is the question that is never asked. When in doubt, attack your fears. God has the answers.

A third type of fear is the fear of giving up our piece of this world. Again, Paul in 2 Timothy gave us guidance. In chapter two of that book, Paul admonished us to be good soldiers in the service of Christ: "Share in suffering as a good soldier of Christ Jesus. No soldier gets entangled in civilian pursuits, since his aim is to please the one that enlisted him."[11] When we become too attached to the things of this world, we cannot be true soldiers of Christ. Just as a soldier headed off to battle takes only those items most vital to accomplishing his mission, so the dedicated Christian should minimize his attachment to the things of this world to allow maximum flexibility in his ability to serve the Lord.

The best response to the problem of fear and shame is to know God. When we have a close personal relationship with our Creator, there is little chance that we will as readily deny our relationship. I call once again on the wisdom of Paul and his advice to Timothy: "But I am not ashamed, for I know whom I have believed, and I am convinced that he is able to guard until that Day what has been entrusted to me."[12] The closer our relationship with the Lord, the stronger our beliefs will be, and the stronger our resolve to acknowledge Him as our Savior and King over our lives.

Knowing God provides us with an eternal perspective on life. When we can keep our priorities in life in order, we are in a much better position to be bold servants of the Lord. We won't succumb as easily to the fears of uncertainty and maintaining our earthly reputations. Where fear and shame are like a cancer that eats away at our ability to lead a dynamic life, knowing and fearing God are the cure.

The ability to partake in periodic retreats provides the opportunity to confront our fears and conquer our feeling of shame. The opportunity to spend concentrated time in study and growth in our love of God can establish habits that will last us throughout the year.

Summary

We live in a fallen world, although God has promised us the strength to overcome the temptations of this world. First Corinthians 10:13 tells us, "No temptation has overtaken you that is not common to man. God is faithful, and he will not let you be tempted beyond your ability, but with temptation, he will also provide the way of escape, that you may be able to endure it." This chapter outlined some of these common temptations. The opportunity to practice spiritual retreat is one of those ways to escape.

When you look up the definition of retreat, you may be tempted to just think of it just as a place to rest or retire. However, the more appropriate way to look at is in the military sense. In battle, one army may retreat for strategic reasons. They may be out-manned or out-maneuvered. However, the objective of the retreat is to refresh and rearm so that when the next battle occurs, the chances for victory are enhanced. We are fighting a mighty Enemy, and we need to be just as well armed as the soldier is in Ephesians 6:11.[13]

We also recognize that something about this world is not quite right. We realize that this is not really our home.[14] We have a sense of discomfort and awkwardness about our daily lives. The obligations and cares of this world do not allow us to live our lives as focused on the Lord and His work as we might want. The opportunity to remove ourselves for a few days allows us to lead a life closer to what Christ modeled for us. Dorothy Bass describes this opportunity in her preface to her book *Practicing Our Faith*.[15]

> Every summer, my family visits a retreat center high in the mountains. My husband delights in the hiking and fishing; I thrive on the absence of phones, televisions, and grocery stores; and the children revel in the freedom they have to roam about unsupervised in a small, safe, mostly outdoor community of friends. All of us enjoy the natural splendor of this place. But there is also something stronger and deeper that keeps us going

back, something harder to describe. When we are there, we slip into a way of life that comes pretty close to our vision of how things are supposed to be. As staff members, we work; we consume appropriately, eating lower on the food chain and doing without the goods and gadgets that usually clutter our lives; we worship daily. In other words, we enter a community shaped by shared practices that make sense, and as we adjust to them we feel ourselves becoming a little different, a little better.[16]

No one seems to question the need for periodic vacations from our earthly work. For many families, this time away from the routine of life is highly anticipated and planned for months in advance. Yet as beneficial as time away from our jobs may be to physically rejuvenate us, how much more beneficial might a time away to reflect on the bigger picture of life be to rejuvenate our soul?

Hopefully this chapter has convinced you that the answer to "Who needs retreat?" is simple. Everyone does, and in particular, you do. But before proceeding directly to the question of "What comprises a true spiritual retreat?" it will be beneficial to examine the historical context of retreat as part of our Christian faith.

Chapter 2: Why Is Retreat Lacking in The Protestant Community?

In chapter one we reviewed some of the root causes that impact everyone in modern society and hamper our ability to lead the dynamic, spirit-filled life that most desire. Unquestionably the culture around us drags us toward unbelief. This cultural pull manifests itself in our desire to be entertained and avoid the potential of boredom in our routine. In addition, our still fallen sin nature continues to drag us back to fear and even shame about our faith. Protestants in general (and evangelicals in particular) have even further challenges when it comes to accepting the need to retreat in our lives. This chapter will look at three of these additional pressures—lack of historical perspective, rewarding activity over contemplation, and a lack of understanding about our spiritual nature.

Lack of Historical Perspective

One of the more astute observations made about church history appeared in a 1975 *Peanuts* comic strip. In the first frame Sally Brown is sitting at her desk, and her brother Charlie is watching her and asking her what she is doing. She responds in frame two that she has to write a paper on church history. Frame three shows the paper with the words "When writing about church history, we have to go back to the very beginning." The final frame continues with the words "Our pastor was born in 1930."[17]

Unfortunately, for too many Christians, this accurately reflects their understanding of the history and traditions of their faith. As a result, many of us miss out on the rich heritage that represents our common Christian background. By not having an understanding of the basic tenants that compose our faith, we are relegated to a living a life that fails to avail itself of hundreds of years of lessons learned by those who preceded us. As the cartoon illustrates, we only know what we have experienced firsthand within the confines of our own individual church background.

Evangelicals in particular can be subject to this compressed view of the history of their faith and the rich traditions that it represents. Again, in a book that is primarily focused on the practice of spiritual retreat, any treatment of church history is going to be cursory at best. However, let us take a look at some of the significant milestones that formed what has become known as the Protestant Christian community.

For many Christians, their understanding of the history of their faith may go back a little further than the history of their particular church (as depicted in the *Peanuts* cartoon above), but there is typically a huge gap in their knowledge and appreciation of church history as a whole. Before analyzing that gap, it might be helpful to have a few working definitions to assist in further discussion.

Protestantism: Defined in the broadest sense, Protestants are those adherents of the Christian faith that have been separated from the Catholic Church since the Reformation. This would include those in the Reformed, Lutheran, Anglican, Anabaptist, Baptist, Methodist, and Presbyterian denominations and a host of other, smaller ones.[18] For the purposes of our discussion, this is the broadest of the terms in our definition pool.

Fundamentalism: Generally, a *fundamentalism* is utilized to identify a movement organized in the early twentieth century to defend orthodox Protestant Christianity against the challenges of theological liberalism.[19] In particular, fundamentalists stand in opposition to higher criticism of

the Bible, believe in a literal interpretation of the Bible (in particular
the Genesis account of creation), and follow a "dispensational"[20] view
of the Bible. Although the term also holds more recent connotations
of political activism for conservative causes, as used in this book, the
primary focus is on the theological implications.

Evangelicalism: Historically, the term *evangelicalism* can trace origins to
late seventeenth century and became an organized movement around
1730 with the emergence of the Methodists in England and the Pietists
among Lutherans in Germany and Scandinavia. According to *The
Institute for the Study of Evangelicalism* website,[21]

> British historian David Bebbington approaches evangelicalism
> from this direction and notes four specific hallmarks of evangelical
> religion: conversionism, the belief that lives need to be changed;
> activism, the expression of the gospel in effort; Biblicism, a
> particular regard for the Bible; and "crucicientrism," a stress
> on sacrifice of Christ on the cross. Bebbington's definition has
> become a standard baseline for most scholars.

Prior to the second half of the twentieth century, the terms *evangelicalism*
and *fundamentalism* were largely synonymous.[22] Beginning in the
1950s, largely due to the ecumenical evangelism of Billy Graham,
evangelicalism began to downplay the direct attacks on liberalism and
focused more on outreach and conversion. Traditional fundamentalists
remained more vocal critics of the "liberal agenda."[23]

The primary point of defining the terms is that almost every Christian
(other than Roman Catholic or Greek Orthodox) will fit somewhere
within the three categories of mainline Protestant, fundamentalist, or
evangelical. Moreover, the church you attend will fit within one of these
three categories, and therefore the affinity toward the distinctive of those
churches will drive much of your understanding of church history. Simply
stated, for many Christians today, their understanding church history has
a gap in it. Effectively, their study of history ends with the end of the

New Testament and commences again on October 31, 1517, with the posting of the *Ninety-Five Theses* by Martin Luther on the church door at Wittenberg. The intervening 1,500 years are effectively ignored by many Christians. In fact, the problem has the potential to be even more acute among fundamentalists and evangelicals, who may be inclined to view "their" history as really only being a product of the twentieth century.

Although this is a gross oversimplification of the topic, the logic proceeds along the following line. If the Protestant Reformation is an improvement on the Roman Catholic Church, then the fundamentalists are an improvement over the mainline Protestant church, which is then further refined by the evangelical movement. Our modern mindset is geared to think this way. In our technological age, surely the next version of the smartphone or computer is better than the prior generation. Why would we stick with old technology when it comes to our entertainment or health care choices? Studying old technology surely is a waste of time! How could that be any different when it comes to understanding our theological history?

As we will see in the next couple of chapters, far from being a waste of time, a deep understanding of the history of our Christian faith can serve to introduce us to practices and thoughts that will deepen our own spirituality and make our daily walks more relevant and Christlike. When we dismiss the historical underpinnings of our creeds and doctrine, we are prone to drift just like a ship loosened from its moorings. Simply stated, we lack perspective, and we are prone to follow the latest popular self-help author.

A pastor once told me, "I don't trust anyone under two hundred years of age. If someone writes something that is really relevant and impactful, it will withstand the scrutiny of time. I don't think we can afford to follow the latest craze, because we will just get whipsawed, following one trend and then another, and we will never mature in our faith." Unfortunately, too many Christians are prone to only read the latest release from a high-profile name in the religious community. By following the "latest is best" mentality, we are ignoring a reservoir of writings and guidance that can impact our lives in a meaningful way.

Rewarding Action over Contemplation

When my children were growing up in the 1980s and 1990s, I remember there was a series of videos advertised called something like *Heroes of the Bible*. Intrigued by the possibility of finding something of more value than what was being offered on television, I requested a catalog.

However, after reviewing the offerings, I realized that this company had "Americanized" their Bible heroes. They had the story of David, but this wasn't the David that was a "man after God's own heart."[24] This was David in his conflict with Goliath. Daniel was in the series as well. However, instead of the Daniel of Daniel 1:20 where King Nebuchadnezzar states, "In every matter of wisdom and understanding about which the king inquired of them, he found them ten times better than the magicians and enchanters that were in all his kingdom." Rather it was the story of Daniel in the lion's den.

The headline of the catalog was the story of Samson. However, what do you really learn when you study the story of Samson?[25] He is pretty much dead space from the neck up. The only real value of the story of Samson is that it demonstrates that no matter how badly you mess up your life, in the end, God can use you for good. Yet he was an American hero. He had big biceps and could create mass mayhem with the makeshift weapon of the jawbone of an ass.

Unfortunately, this is just another indication of how culture has inculcated our faith. We live in a culture that honors activity and visible accomplishments. The busier someone is, the more respect he or she tends to receive from those around him or her. After all, aren't busy people important people—getting busier as they get more important?

This attitude has carried itself over in to our spiritual lives as well. Review the definition above of David Bebbington of evangelicalism. Tenet number two is activism—the expression of the gospel in effort. Granted, "Faith without works is dead."[26] However, there is more to understanding our faith then just as a motivation for good actions. This attitude toward physical activity over and above a more spiritual and contemplative life also owes some of its fervor to this "Protestant work ethic" and warrants some further discussion.

The concept of the Protestant work ethic was formalized in the study of German sociologist Max Weber. In 1905 he published his thesis in *The Protestant Ethic and the Spirit of Capitalism.*[27] Weber theorized that there is an affinity between early modern capitalism and Calvinism. In particular, Christians were inculcated to work hard in their secular calling in order to demonstrate their salvation. In recent times, the term has been given the broader meaning as a tendency to work hard as a way of proving one's self-worth, along with a residual Puritanical thought that casts suspicion on excessive leisure.[28]

Coupled with the culture at large that rewards activism, it is easy to understand how many (or most) Christians view the contemplative lifestyle as somehow inferior to one filled with action and activity. However, this is not an either-or situation. Above all, as Christians we are commanded to "love the Lord God with all our heart, soul, mind and strength."[29] It is possible to view loving God with our strength as calling for an outward action. However, loving with our heart, soul, and mind appears to have a particularly inward and contemplative aspect about it. Again, spending time in spiritual retreat can serve to strengthen a believer and make him or her that much more effective in accomplishing the outward activities that God has led him or her to pursue. Without the time away to reflect on the spiritual aspects of our lives in Christ, we risk the activities we pursue being of our own choosing instead of our Lord's leading.

A significant part of the reason for pursuit of activity over contemplation is the general lack of understanding of our spiritual nature. It is with that in mind that we turn to that aspect of why Protestants don't understand the necessity of spiritual retreat in our lives.

Lack of Understanding of Our Spiritual Nature

We are unique in God's creation. No other creature has a spirit nature. Yet many in today's world tend to be more focused on addressing our physical nature and pay scant attention to our spiritual health. This attitude can be traced to some of the issues already discussed. The privatization of religion to just a matter of personal conviction can trivialize the complexity of the true nature of our beings as creatures made in the image of our Creator. In addition, the penchant we have toward activity over contemplation can dull our sensitivity to our spiritual nature. An outward focus on action limits the energy and time we have to contemplate our inward being. The lack of historical perspective doesn't harken us back to an earlier time when the clear focus on spiritual growth as a matter integral to our Christian maturity was self-evident.

As we will discuss in a later chapter on the story of Christian spirituality, there is a rich tradition to draw upon in this area that is applicable to Protestants. However, a preliminary understanding of this critical element of our being can be examined merely by spending a few minutes examining the role of spirituality in "mainline" Protestant churches vis-à-vis our Roman Catholic and Greek Orthodox brethren—those who represent what we view as having a "high church" liturgy.

What is the structure of most Protestant religious services? There are usually a couple of songs to begin the service, followed by announcements and then an offering, a sermon, and then a closing song. The primary focus is often on the message given by the minister or pastor. Depending on the denomination, the tone of the message can be preaching or teaching. The theme can be a call to personal salvation, to social action, or maybe to personal application of biblical principles to your life. Although the pattern in most churches is relatively fixed from Sunday to Sunday, the themes vary, and certainly repetition of content is frowned upon. The pastor who delivers the same message in exactly the same way won't stay in his position for long in a society that is hooked on highly professionalized media content delivery.

With many of today's Protestant megachurches, there is a premium placed upon sophisticated delivery of music and the outstanding oratory skills of the pastor. Each phase of the service needs to be choreographed, and transitions happen in a seamless fashion. What is often lacking is the personal involvement of the individual parishioner. Many times the individual in the pew is the passive recipient of content—not substantially different than if he or she were sitting in an auditorium and observing a theatrical play. There are no uncomfortable pauses where the congregant is called upon to sit and reflect on his or her individual spirituality. There are not periods of rote repetition of phrases that might require the person to think deeply on their own about the meaning and purpose behind the ancient wording that has been passed from generation to generation. In short, the nature of our church services has taken on the nature of our society as a whole—highly professionalized content delivery that has direct application and relevancy to addressing one's particular needs.

Let us contrast the nature of the Roman Catholic Mass to the typical Protestant service. The basic structure of the Mass can be accounted for in five parts (or rites).[30]

(1) Introductory Rites: After the priest enters the sanctuary (often accompanied by a deacon and altar servers) he invites the congregants to partake in an act of penitence. "Kyrie, eleison" ("Lord, have mercy") is sung or said, followed by "Gloria in excelsis Deo" ("Glory to God in the highest"). Both of these are ancient praises dating back centuries.

(2) Liturgy of the Word: On Sundays and special church days, three readings of Scripture are made. On other days only two are read. The first reading is from the Old Testament and is usually accompanied by the reading of a Psalm. The second reading is from the New Testament (typically a Pauline epistle). The third reading is typically from one of the gospels and read by a deacon or the priest. These readings are typically followed by a short homily or sermon that reflects on some aspect of the day's readings. Although the homily is prepared by the local priest, the readings are uniform throughout the church. This section of the Mass is then concluded by a group recitation of the Apostles' Creed.

(3) Liturgy of the Eucharist: Where in most Protestant denominations the emphasis of the service is around the sermon, in the Catholic tradition the celebration of the Eucharist (Holy

Communion) is the focus of the service.[31] The liturgy of the Eucharist begins with the ceremonial placing of gifts of bread and wine on the altar. There then follows a series of prayers to consecrate the communion elements. These prayers include exhortations that the gifts are offered in the power of the Holy Spirit (epiclesis) and a recollection of the words and actions of Jesus at the Last Supper (institution narrative and consecration). Immediately after the consecration, the priest displays the communion elements and says, "The mystery of faith," and the people respond back using one of three prescribed formulae.

(4) Communion Rite: This section of the Mass begins with the recitation of the Lord's Prayer. The priest then states another short prayer (embolism), and the people respond with the doxology. The sign of peace is exchanged, and then "Lamb of God" ("Agnus Dei") is sung, and the priest breaks the host and places a piece in the chalice containing the wine. The priest then presents the transubstantiated elements to the congregation and states, "Behold the Lamb of God, behold him who takes away the sin of the world. Blessed are those called to the supper of the Lamb." Then all repeat, "Lord, I am not worthy that you should enter under my roof, but only say the word and my soul shall be healed."[32] The priest then distributes Communion to the people who approach the altar in procession fashion.

(5) Concluding Rite: The priest or deacon dismisses the people using one of four prescribed formulas, to which the congregation responds, "Thanks be to God."

Even the above cursory review of the Roman Catholic Mass should make it evident that the tone and emphasis of the Catholic service is distinctly different from most Protestant services. Embedded in the Mass are traditional elements that date to the earliest years of the church.

There is a sense of history in realizing that the words and actions of today's congregants parallel those of Catholics of centuries ago (with the exception of the use of English instead of Latin). There is significant emphasis on the mystery of the Eucharist as the focal point of the service. Without commenting on the doctrine of transubstantiation (the bread and wine actually become the body and blood of Christ), there is a feeling of proximity of Jesus Christ, and the emphasis on the mystical relationship between savior and parishioner is evident. This mystical relationship only becomes more pronounced when we look at the Eastern Orthodox tradition.

Where the structure and content of the Roman Catholic mass remains relatively constant throughout the year, the Eastern Orthodox Church follow a rigid but constantly changing annual schedule. There are services that exist for each day of the year and contain both a fixed segment and changing elements depending on the day. Typically the local church only holds services on weekends and holy days. Unlike Protestant (or even Roman Catholic) services, Eastern Orthodox services are not relegated to one fixed meeting. In fact, the standard services are actually composed of six cycles that encompass the entire day. The traditional daily cycle of services is as follows:[33]

(1) Vespers—sundown, the beginning of the liturgical day;

(2) Compline—after the evening meal and prior to bedtime;

(3) Midnight office—prayer time usually only practiced in monasteries;

(4) Matins—first service in the morning, usually starting before sunrise;

(5) Divine liturgy—the Eucharist service; and

(6) Hours—first, third, sixth and ninth. These are separate times of prayer that can be sung at the appropriate hours or can be sung in the aggregate for convenience sake. The traditional

time would require first hour to be sung prior to matins, third and sixth hour to be sung prior to the Divine Liturgy, and the ninth hour prior to vespers.

The Divine Liturgy is the celebration of the Eucharist. As part of the service, a number of small items are brought to the altar, including a gold or silver chalice with red wine, a small urn of warm water, a metallic communion spoon, a small metallic spear, a sponge, a metal disk with cut pieces of bread, and a star-shaped piece of metal for carrying the elements. Also found on the altar is the antimins, a silk cloth signed by the appropriate diocesan bishop, upon which the sanctification of the holy elements takes place during the Divine Liturgy.

There are three Divine Liturgies that are in common use in the Eastern Orthodox Church:

(1) The Divine Liturgy of Saint John Chrysostom used on most days of the year

(2) The Divine Liturgy of Saint Basil the Great, which is used on the five Sundays of Lent and select other holy days

(3) The Divine Liturgy of Saint James of Jerusalem celebrated once a year on the feast day of Saint James

The format of the Divine Liturgy is fixed, although the specific readings and hymns vary depending on the time of year. While arrangements may vary slightly, the Divine Liturgy will always consist of three interrelated parts:

(1) The liturgy of preparation, which includes the entry and vesting prayers

(2) The liturgy of the Word, also called the liturgy of the Catechumens because in ancient times those new to the faith

and in a period of training were allowed to attend. This segment consists of opening blessings, a series of litanies (prayers), antiphon (scriptural readings), and supplemental readings from the Epistles and gospels.

(3) The liturgy of the faithful (available to only baptized members of the church in good standing). This segment includes additional prayers and hymns as well as the recitation of the Nicene Creed. This is also the time when the Eucharist is celebrated through the remembrance of Christ's incarnation, death, and resurrection. The call is made to the Holy Spirit to change the elements of bread and wine into the body and blood of Christ.[34]

Orthodox services are sung nearly in their entirety. Because the human voice is considered the most perfect instrument of praise, musical instruments are not usually present. There has developed a relatively sophisticated set of tones or modes that are utilized by the choirs, and in American services it is not unusual for the choirs to learn multiple styles and sing them in multiple languages, including English, Russian, and Greek.[35]

The use of incense is also another common denominator among Eastern Orthodox churches. Traditionally frankincense is the base of the incense, and it represents the sweetness of the prayers of the congregants rising up to God. The incense is burned in an ornate golden censer that hangs at the end of three chains representing the Trinity.[36]

A third distinctive practice is that of fasting within the Orthodox Church. In fact, between religious holidays and other seasons of fasting, an adherent to Eastern Orthodoxy could participate in some level of fasting for nearly half the year. In general, fasting means abstention from meat, dairy products, eggs, fish, wine, and olive oil. For those inclined, a full fast from all types of foods is not uncommon. Church regulations on the length of the fast are provided, but generally Wednesdays and Fridays are days of fasting. As discussed later in this book in the chapter on spiritual disciplines, fasting is seen as a way to discipline the body from carnal temptations and to lead a more Christlike life. [37]

A final attribute to be examined is the role of icons in the Orthodox Church. *Icon* comes from the Greek word for *image*. The style of icons is fairly formulaic, as they are designed to convey information about the person being depicted. The role of icons is specifically defined under canonical law. They are not objects of worship, but rather serve as a point of focus of worship of the object or person depicted. An analogy might be that when you kiss the picture of a loved one, you are not showing affection toward the picture, but rather the person depicted in the picture. Regarding the commandment not to make idols, the Orthodox Church's logic is that before Christ became incarnate, any depiction of God would be blasphemous. However, once God incarnate arrived in the form of Jesus, depiction became possible.[38]

To those individuals who have grown up in a Protestant denomination, many of the practices cited above such as incense, chants, the use of icons, and fasts can seem alien at best and blasphemous at worst. This might be our attitude in particular given the justifiably strongly held belief that salvation is a gift from God and not as a result of our works.[39] However, objectively speaking, adherence to these ancient practices can have the impact of sensitizing a follower of Christ to the strong spiritual connection that should be a part of every believer's life. A disregard of our spiritual nature can lead to an incomplete appreciation of our relationship with God. Again, Mark 12:30 admonishes us to love the Lord with all of our heart, soul, mind, and strength. In other words, we must love the Lord with all that we are, and that most certainly requires a love that emanates from a strong spiritual connection with our heavenly father.

Summary

The lack by many Protestants and in particular many evangelicals of a deep appreciation for the spiritual side of our relationship with God is a function of many variables. Many of us lack an appreciation of our historical past and truncate our knowledge of the history of Christianity by starting with the Reformation. In fact, we may even carry over a cultural bias that progress is only forward and that reflecting back to the practices and people of the past could only lead to a regression in our spiritual growth. We live in a society that places a premium on action and any activity (or perceived lack of activity) that requires us to still ourselves and "passively" reflect on the deeper spiritual things of life is potentially a self-indulgent waste of time. This lack of historical perspective and cultural penchant toward activity can easily result in a lack of a complete understanding of our spiritual nature. We fail to value the critical importance that should be placed on growing this element of our relationship with our spiritual Creator.

In a very elementary way, Protestants can see how we have been impacted as described above by spending some time understanding how the Roman Catholic and Eastern Orthodox Churches approach their religious services. Even the cursory review of these two church's practices can yield some obvious contrast in approach to worship. Protestant denominations focus primarily on the teaching or preaching time in church on Sunday mornings, thus appealing to the mind and potentially the heart. These high church denominations appear to have much more of a focus on renewing and refreshing the soul. At this point I should clarify that I am not indicating that everyone should convert from Protestantism to Catholicism or Orthodoxy. Rather, I am trying to lay the groundwork for further study of what exists within these denominations background that appeal to the spiritual side of our nature. By having an appreciation of those historical distinctive, as Protestants we can judiciously borrow or assimilate those for our own spiritual growth and the critical nature that personal retreat has in that growth.

If you plug "spiritual retreat" in to your web browser, around 80 percent of the sites that come up are representative of the Roman Catholic or Eastern Orthodox faith. They come out of the deep tradition these churches have in the concept of spiritual retreat. What we as Protestants and in particular evangelicals need to remember is that our heritage for the first 1,500 years of our faith is common with these traditions. We as Protestants appear to have thrown out the baby with the bathwater when it comes to acknowledging our deep history in retreat. This is particularly true when you gain an understanding that many of the practices that Martin Luther and others were protesting about found kindred spirits in those of the Catholic and Orthodox traditions, who were on the forefront of the emphasis on personal piety and spiritual retreat. It is with this in mind that the next couple of chapters will focus on these individuals who laid the groundwork for our heritage of nurturing the spiritual side of our nature.

Chapter 3: The Emergence of the Monastic Movement

To understand the development of the concepts of personal spirituality and retreat, it is important to understand the development of the monastic movement. To appreciate the factors that created the emergence of the monastic movement, it is important to understand a watershed moment in the history of the Christian church. That moment was the ascendancy of Constantine the Great to rulership of the Roman Empire.

Constantine the Great

A quick review of the status of the Christian faith in society from the end of the apostolic era to the arrival of Constantine will set the stage for an appreciation of his impact on Christian history. In keeping with the Great Commission,[40] the Christian faith began to spread across the Mediterranean Basin, starting with the events at Pentecost.[41] Initially, although strongly opposed by the Jewish leaders, the Christian faith had not drawn the focus of the Roman emperor. To the outsider, it appeared to be just another Jewish sect and therefore more of an internal Jewish issue. Indeed, even the early Christians did not believe they were followers of a new religion. They were just Jews who believed the prophecy of the Messiah had been fulfilled in Jesus Christ.[42]

In AD 54 Nero ascended to the emperorship of Rome. Although initially a competent ruler, he eventually became infatuated with the grandeur and power of his role and became despised by the populace. In AD 64 a massive fire broke out in Rome that lasted for a week and eventually destroyed ten of the fourteen sections of the city. Rumors began to circulate that Nero himself had actually started the fire to provide him the opportunity to rebuild Rome in his image. (The reality is that Nero was several miles away when the fire broke out and there has never been any evidence that he directed the arson.)[43] To throw suspicion off himself, he needed a scapegoat. Two of the boroughs that had not burned had a significant population of Jews and Christians. In general there was a growing suspicion of this "Jewish sect." Many false rumors had been circulating about "abominations" that occurred during their worship services, so Nero accused the Christians of setting the fires. Thus began the first wave of persecution of this religion in its infancy.

Over the next 250 years, Christians were subject to periodic waves of persecutions by the Roman emperors. The most common cause was the failure of Christians to conform to the practice of emperor worship and other perceived "civil duties." Persecutions continued throughout the second century under multiple emperors. Christians could often escape punishment merely by acknowledging the emperor or other Roman gods in addition to their own God. Some Christians did so, but many remained faithful and went to their deaths instead of recanting. The stories of these early martyrs served as an inspiration to many that were to follow them. Individuals such as Polycarp and Justin Martyr set standards that were an example for generations to follow about adherence to the precepts of the Christian faith.

Early in the fourth century, the last and greatest persecution began under the Roman Emperor Diocletian. He had reorganized the administration of the empire by dividing it in to four districts, each with its own ruler, with Diocletian retaining ultimate authority. By this time there were several converts to Christianity in the Roman army. Diocletian viewed this as a potential threat, as he saw that their allegiance to him was not absolute. These Christian soldiers were required to recant their faith and when they failed to do so, many were put to death. The situation grew worse. Virtually any event that negatively impacted the empire was attributed to the Christians and provided another opportunity to expand the persecution.

Eventually Diocletian's health caused him to abdicate, and political chaos broke out as the four regional rulers jockeyed for position as the supreme ruler. One of those rulers was Constantine, who had ascended to the role of ruler of the Western portion of the empire upon the death of his father, Constantius Chlorus. There is evidence that Constantine's mother was in fact a Christian, and as such, Constantine saw the persecutions occurring throughout the rest of the empire as unjust. For that and other more political reasons, Constantine marched on Rome to secure his position as the ultimate ruler of the empire.

According to historical chroniclers, Constantine had a dream that if he placed the Christian symbol on the shields of his soldiers, he would be victorious in battle. At the battle of the Milvian Bridge, Constantine was victorious over his principal rival Maxentius, and shortly thereafter he consolidated his control and ascended to the role of Caesar.[44] Almost overnight the status of Christianity went from that of an outlaw religion to one that was virtually state sponsored. Conversion to the Christian faith became increasingly popular among the elite. As one church historian stated:

> Over against those ... who saw the more recent events as the fulfillment of God's purpose, there were those who bewailed what they saw as the low level to which Christian life had descended. The narrow gate of which Jesus had spoken had become so wide that countless multitudes were hurrying past it—some seemingly after privilege and position, without caring to delve too deeply into the meaning of Christian baptism and life under the cross. Bishops competed against each other after prestigious positions. The rich and powerful seemed to dominate the life of the church. The tares were growing so rapidly that they threatened to choke out the wheat.[45]

During the periods of persecution, many of the early Christians had held fast to their faith, even during times of great persecution. Many of these "sincere" Christians became concerned about the impact that personal peace and affluence might have on the church free of the fires of persecution that had served to cleanse and purify it. What were individuals who had these concerns to do? Again, quoting Gonzalez:

> Many found the answer in the monastic life; to flee from human society, to leave everything behind, to dominate the body and its passions, which gave way to temptation. Thus at the very time when churches in large cities were flooded by thousands demanding baptism, there was a veritable exodus of other thousands that sought beatitude in solitude."[46]

Supporting the monastic ideal was a fundamental belief that the body was a fallen container for the soul and that an individual could not mature in his faith until he could overcome the temptations of the flesh. The passions of our humanness had to be controlled, and discipline of the body was necessary to accomplish that. There was also the adherence to the apostle Paul's admonition to lead the celibate life so that a singular focus on the Lord could occur. It was also felt that the monastic life was one of isolation. In fact the word *monk* derives from the Greek word *monachos*, which translates as *solitary*.[47]

The monastic movement was born, although who actually can claim the status as father of the movement will likely never be known. What we do have available are writings about an early monk named Anthony that can give us some insights in to the emergence of the monastic movement.

The Life and Letters of Anthony

Anthony was an Egyptian who lived in the first half of the fourth century. He died in AD 356 and at his death, Athanasius, the bishop of Alexandria, wrote an account of Anthony's heroic struggles against the temptation of demons.[48] As was typical of the early monks, Anthony sought separation from the world around him by departing for the desert. Thus Antony and others like him were deemed "the desert fathers."

According to Athanasius account, Anthony was born to a well-to-do farming family on the left bank of the Nile. His parents died young, and Anthony and his sister inherited a large tract of land that would provide a comfortable life for both of them. However, he was convicted by the messages in the gospels that called for followers of Christ to give up all and follow him. Abandoning his wealth, he moved out of the city and began a life of increasing asceticism. Often he was plagued by attacks from demons that sought to have him abandon this life of sacrifice, prayer, and contemplation. As the account is written, often these attacks resulted in physical injury that would leave Anthony near death.

At age thirty-five he abandoned the inhabited portions of Egypt for the desert. After crossing the Nile he located an old fort on the mountain of Pispar, where he isolated himself. For twenty years he did not see another individual. The story of his great holiness spread, and over the years a collection of hermits took up residence in the caves around Anthony's residence. At the constant request of these other hermits, he broke his period of isolation and emerged to teach and organize the others. Eventually, he founded the monastery Der Mar Antonios (which is still in existence), where he spent another forty years in semi-isolation, emerging occasionally to speak to visitors. According to Saint Jerome, he died at the age of 105 and had two of his disciples bury him at an unknown location.[49]

Besides the semibiographical story of Anthony's life by Athanasius, Anthony himself dictated seven letters that still exist and give us insights into his life and philosophy. Anthony's letters provide his theoretical and theological basis for the aesthetic life. His ideas appear to be based on the writings of third-century theologian Origen. In broad terms, all of God's creatures were at one time equal spiritual beings, but after a falling away from God, certain creations were given human form. The body was fallen and prone to sin, but with sufficient empowerment by the Holy Spirit, the temptation of the flesh could be overcome.[50]

Although Anthony may be given special recognition as one of the early desert monks, he was far from alone in his quest for spiritual retreat far from the cities. In fact, some travelers who visited the desert regions of Egypt were quick to comment that the desert was becoming more populated than many of the cities, with over thirty thousand men and women living in one region alone.[51] By and large, they all lived lives of simplicity, often living off of minimal substance in small gardens they would grow. Many also resorted to basket weaving, as the required material of reeds was readily available, and this activity had the added benefit of allowing ample time for prayer, meditation, and spiritual reflection.

Over a period of time a rift developed between many of these early monks and the established Catholic Church. From the monk's perspective, the priests and bishops who lived in the city in opulence and increasing earthly power were moving further away from the simple life advocated by Jesus Christ. From the bishop's point of view, the monks represented fanatics who failed to adhere to many of the established doctrines of the church. Many of the monks had not received any formal training on theology and were prone to straying from orthodox positions. At times in the fifth century this even led to episodes of violence between the two groups.[52]

Pachomius and Communal Living

Over a period of time, these monks began to congregate for the purposes of instruction and the celebration of communion. It would be impossible to identify the father of this type of communal living. However, a monk named Pachomius can be given credit for being the organizer who gave form to this type of spiritual living arrangements.

Pachomius was born in AD 286 in a small village in southern Egypt. Although born to pagan parents, Pachomius encountered Christians during his years in the army and was so impressed by their love for others that he converted to Christianity upon his discharge. Some years later, he made the decision to withdraw to the desert, where he came under the tutelage of an old monk. According to legend, he heard a voice commanding him to leave and set up an enclosure large enough for several monks to inhabit. He recruited others to join him. Initially, the recruits were unable to live in community as Pachomius had hoped, and he expelled this initial class. He determined that some of the military principles he had learned in the army had applicability in a community such as this. He outlined certain fundamental rules that everyone needed to agree to if they were to join his new community. Chief among those were obedience to superiors, the abandonment of any privately owned property, and an equal sharing in the physical tasks of maintaining the community.[53]

Pachomius's community was very successful. During his lifetime, nine additional communities were established, and his sister Mary founded similar communities for women. All of the monasteries consisted of a similar physical layout with a single entrance to a walled compound. Within the walls were multiple structures to house bakeries, weaving rooms, storehouses, and meeting halls. The monks were given rooms that would hold two individuals each.

The daily routines were fixed as well among the individual communities. They consisted of periods of work and prayer. In fact, Paul's admonition to pray without ceasing was taken literally, as all of the monks were advised to pray as they worked at their humble tasks. Although the monks had no possessions and lived very humbly, they did not practice extreme asceticism. They would often sell the excess they produced to have sufficient funds to aid the poor travelers who would show up at their gate. In fact, many of those that showed up eventually sought to join the group. This was not easily accomplished, as those seeking admission were first required to beg at the front gate for several days. As such they demonstrated both strength of conviction regarding their chosen path as well as a willingness to follow in obedience to the elder monks.[54]

The leadership of the group had a well-defined hierarchical structure. Each housing unit had a superior who was in charge of those under his direct care. These unit superiors then reported to Pachomius and his successors. Pachomius established the tradition of naming his own successor, to whom all the monks in the monastery pledged their allegiance.[55]

Although the monastic movement may have found fertile soul in the deserts of Egypt, it did not remain unique to this geographic area. The ideals of monastic living spread throughout the Roman Empire. One of the more well known of this next generation of monks was Martin of Tours.

Martin of Tours

Throughout the eastern portion of the Roman Empire, monks were setting up residence in numerous places. Several of these monks were well known for their exaggerated ascetic life (such as living on top of a column). However, the real contribution did not come from those who isolated themselves in a hermit type of existence, but rather those who served as witnesses to a more Christlike life in daily living to the greater church body. Among those who had the greatest impact as both church leaders and monastics was Bishop Martin of Tours.

Martin was born in AD 316 in what is now Hungary. The *Life of Saint Martin*,[56] written by Sulpitius Severus, was widely read for centuries and helped shape the monastic life in the West. According to this biography, Martin was the son of a tribune in the Roman horse guard. At age ten, he entered the Christian faith and studied to become baptized. Although now an accepted religion, Christianity was still not prominent, and his father, to discourage his son, had him enlisted in the army at age fifteen before he had completed his catechism. Martin was later deployed to Gaul (now France), where he experienced a unique vision that became a defining moment in his life. As Martin was approaching the gates of the city of Amien, he saw a nearly naked beggar freezing in the cold. Martin impulsively took his sword and cut his cloak in half, giving part of it to the beggar. Later that night, he had a dream where the partial cloak was being worn by Jesus Christ, who said, "Look upon Martin, the unbaptized soldier who has clad me." When Martin awoke, the cloak was amazingly restored to its whole. This confirmed to Martin his piety, and he was baptized at age eighteen.

Martin served in the army another two years but became convinced that he was to be a soldier of Christ and refused to bear arms against the enemy. He was jailed for a short time on charges of cowardice. Martin then offered to go unarmed to the front of the battle. However, the opposing army surprisingly offered to surrender and seek peace, and Martin was released from army service.

Martin established the first monastery in Gaul, and it became a center for the evangelization of the surrounding country. His reputation for holiness spread far and wide, and he was acclaimed the Bishop of Tours, a town near the monastery. He established the rudiments of the parish system and also worked to eliminate the vestiges of paganism in the area. The stories of Martin's good works and kindness became legendary. He continued to spend great amounts of time in prayer in a small cell he had constructed next to his offices.

Later in life, Martin returned to the monastery of Marmoutier, which he had founded. However, monasticism had been changed. Instead of being viewed as a discipline of isolation and separation from those around them, the monks now had an example that a life of charity and concern for those in need could be integrated with a holy life of the practice of spiritual disciplines. In addition, the life of community, together with like-minded individuals, evolved. This necessitated the creation of rules of communal life. One organizer of such communities who was to have a lasting impact was Saint Benedict.

Saint Benedict

The development of Western monasticism owes much of its current structure to Benedict. He was born in Nursia in Italy around AD 480 to a family from the old Roman aristocracy. At age twenty he determined that the life of hermit would be his. According to legend, he lived for three years in a cave in the Simbruini Mountains, about forty miles west of Rome.

As happened with the Egyptian hermits, he eventually gathered several followers, and the space in the mountains proved impractical. Benedict moved the small community to Monte Cassino, a place so remote that it still had a sacred grove where local inhabitants carried on pagan rituals. He ordered the grove cut down and on the same spot constructed a small monastery. His twin sister, Scholastica, settled nearby and founded a similar community for women.[57]

Benedict's greatest remembered contribution was the creation of the *Rule of Saint Benedict*. The document is fairly brief, consisting of only seventy-three short chapters. The content is both of a spiritual nature (advising the adherent how to live a more Christlike life) and organizational, establishing how the monastery should be run. More than half the chapters give advice on how to live a humble life and how to respond when another member of the community does not. Other chapters advise on such things as what the monks should eat and be given in the way of bedding. Two chapters give specific advice to the abbot who will lead the community on how to carry out this responsibility.[58]

There are two consistent themes throughout the rules—permanence and obedience. The first means that once a commitment has been made to join the community, the monk is not free to leave to go to another monastery. The requirement of obedience is both to the *Rule* itself and, strictly and promptly, to the abbot. This obedience is to be not only in action, but also in attitude. If the monk believes the requested task is impossible, he should explain to the abbot his concerns. However, if after discussion the abbot still dictates obedience, the task should be done willingly to the best of the monk's ability.[59]

It is also relevant to note that Benedict's rule departs from the strict asceticism that marked the earlier monastic movements. While the monks of the desert lived on bread, salt, and water, Benedict prescribed two meals a day that would include cooked dishes as well as fruit and vegetables. Each monk was also given a bed with a pillow and cover.

The impact of Benedict on monastic life should not be underestimated. He established a structure that has been adhered to by tens of thousands of individuals over the years and is still the predominate format in use among monasteries around the world. The Benedictine Federation and the Cistercians are both direct descendants of Benedict. The influence of Saint Benedict produced a true spiritual revival in Europe. Over the next several centuries, his followers spread across the continent and established a new cultural unity based on the Christian faith.

Interesting—but Who Cares about a Bunch of "Fanatics"?

Many of you may be saying at this point in time, "That's all very interesting from a historical perspective, but what does the life of some fanatics who lived in caves have to do with my living my life today?" In fact, it may seem like no more than just an odd historical anomaly. Discussing and reviewing the history of monasticism may in fact seem surprisingly discomforting. The trademarks of asceticism, communal living, simplicity of lifestyles, and systematic focus on spiritual practices are almost alien concepts to the twenty-first-century Protestant Christian.

Over the centuries, the practices of simplicity and mutual aid have been expression of the desire for faithful living. The strength of these practices is clearly evident in celibate orders within most religious traditions, whose members share common households and vows of poverty. For many today, this model remains evocative, but does not compellingly translate into the realities of contemporary life.[60]

We have this strange tension that exists in our lives. On one hand, we admire people who seem to lead lives that are "sold out" to the Lord. On the other hand we don't see how such fervor has any practical application in today's complicated and hectic world. The reality of the situation is that many of these practices are exactly what we need to combat the pace of life that we have let culture impose upon us. We will discuss the spiritual disciplines in a later chapter. For now, let's take a look at a couple of the hallmarks of monastic living that appear the most at odds with modern culture and see how a recovery of these attitudes in our lives can improve our spiritual walk. These two attributes are asceticism and simplicity.

Asceticism

Perhaps no other characteristic of the early monastic fathers seems more at odds with modern culture than the idea of denying oneself of any "legitimate" pleasures. It seems anachronistic at best and masochistic at worse. In order to determine why such practices have any applicability to us today, it would be helpful to review why the ancient monks felt it necessary to practice such denials and whether their motivations have any ongoing benefit to Christians today.

If you recall, the earliest desert fathers retreated from a society and a church they believed had grown "soft" and unfocused in the aftermath of the end of persecution with the rise of the reign of Constantine. Arguably. the early hermits may have taken the concept of self-denial to an extreme that has little applicability to today. However, as you review the purposes of such denial as moderated by men such as Benedict, a philosophy emerges that is both enlightening and encouraging.

What might have served as the motivation for an upper-class man to abandon a life of relative luxury for the discipline and sparseness of monastic life? Although certainly not universal, in several well-documented cases it was a sudden experience of a sense of loss that contributed to producing a profound life change.[61] In the case of aristocrat Sulpicius Severus (the author of the biography of Martin of Tours discussed above), it was the death of his wife. Sulpicius had a friend, Paulus Meropius Paulinus, who joined Sulpicius upon the death of his son in the 390s.[62]

Perhaps the most well-known individual who adopted a code of asceticism was the great Christian thinker Augustine of Hippo. As a youth and young adult, Augustine led a life of hedonism. However, after his conversion to Christianity, he adopted a life of strict discipline and denial. His primary influences were the Bishop Ambrose, the account of *The Life of Anthony,* and his own study of the model for Christian living that he saw in the book of Acts.

> For you have read in the Act of the Apostles, they possessed everything in common and distribution to each was made to each in proportion to one's need.[63]

Augustine had a vision for monasticism that was considerably different from the early Egyptian desert fathers. Where they emphasized asceticism for purposes of self-transformation, he viewed the renunciation of individual materialism as necessary for creation of a community held together largely by the bonds of mutual love and friendship (either in a monastic community or as part of the Christian community as a whole). Augustine's vision for the severity of the ascetic life was also more tempered than that exhibited by the hermits of the desert. In Jerome's *Life of Paul the First Hermit*, the desert monks were reported to live as recluses for thirty years, eating only coarse barley bread and drinking muddy water.[64] Augustine envisioned a communal sharing of resources that was limited and certainly not extravagant, but would be designed to ensure good health and the appropriate respect for the body as a creation of God and the temple of the Holy Spirit in this world.[65] It would be this more moderate view of asceticism that would influence subsequent monks and eventually become the basis of Saint Benedict's *Rules* that were discussed above.

Perhaps the best "translation" of the ideas of asceticism as espoused by the early monastic movement can find its modern day equivalent in the concept of simplicity.

Simplicity

Sharon Daloz Parks has written, "The practice of simplicity is an orientation to life that, over time, fosters a sense of right proportion and right relation within the dynamic and interdependent household of the whole earth community. Practicing simplicity is not, however, simple."[66]

This seems even more evident when you think about our attitudes about those religious communities that attempt to practice simplicity in this ever more complicated world. In my section of the state of Indiana, we are close to several Amish communities. For the most part, there is a respect for the lifestyle these communities are seeking to live, but this respect is tempered with skepticism about the "practicality" of avoiding such modern conveniences as electricity and the automobile. Yet, at the same time, all of us yearn for a slower pace of life.

Simplicity does not only encompass a limit on modern conveniences. Simplicity is really an attitude about how one is to live one's life. Too many of us have involved ourselves in too many good things. I remember once reading my wife an introduction I had penned that was going to be used by our pastor to introduce me before I was to preach in our church one Sunday. After an ego-inflating recitation of the numerous boards I served on and awards I had received, my wife simply replied, "It all sounds like a man who doesn't know how to say no!"

Therein may be the link between the monastic movement and its restrictions on possessions and excessive utilization of God's good blessings and how the individual twenty-first-century Christian should lead their lives. We need to learn how to say yes and no utilizing the eternal perspective of Christian Scripture and practices. To make a change in our daily habits doesn't come from just good intentions. We must be purposeful in how we conduct ourselves. To break the cultural pull toward materialism requires a change in practices. In fact, the word *asceticism* comes from the Greek root *askesis*, signifying exercise or training. We must realize that we must consciously deny ourselves things that on the surface seem "fine."

> Having said yes to the acquisition of so many material things, we are unable to say yes to the larger demands of the spirit. Slowly, perhaps even bitterly, we come to realize that we do not own our possessions, they own us.[67]

When one systematically and consciously participates in retreat, one becomes armed to fight back against the pull of this materialistic world. In later chapters we will discuss what true Christian spirituality is and what Christian practices can be exercised to make us more capable of simplifying our lives. However, we are not quite ready to head there yet. There is still more to be learned from the monastic traditions that are a part of our Christian heritage. In the next chapter we will follow the growth of the monastic movement through the medieval period to the present time.

Chapter 4: Monasticism up to Modern Times

Although the *Rule of Saint Benedict* provided guidance and structure for the monastic movement for centuries, the role of monks and monasteries evolved over time. New practices and responsibilities were adopted as world history marched forward. This chapter will provide an overview of some of these key events and people and examine what can be learned as it relates to the Christian today.

The Expansion of Daily Life at the Monastery

Although Benedict himself said little about study, very soon this became a primary occupation of the Benedictine monks. In order to celebrate the divine office (the spiritual readings and exercises set forth in the *Rule*) books became a necessity. Monks became very adept at copying biblical manuscripts as well as other texts and thus helped preserve these literary treasures for subsequent generations.[68] The monasteries slowly evolved into centers for learning. Initially this instruction took place for the benefit of children and young adults that were placed in the monks' care to begin their training to become monks. As will be discussed later in this chapter, from this humble beginning sprang some of the great universities of the world.

Slowly, these monasteries began to have a growing economic impact. By design, many of the monasteries had been built on desolate or marginal land. Eventually, after years of work, the property surrounding the monasteries was brought into useful production, adding significantly to the tillable land of Europe. In addition, the monk's attitude that hard physical labor could be coupled with the great spiritual and intellectual achievement set a new standard for a society where the wealthy and prominent citizenry had disdained physical effort as relegated to the lower socioeconomic class.[69]

The Fall of the Roman Empire

In effect, over time, the monastic orders became centers of stability and civility in a world that was quickly deteriorating. By the beginning of the fourth century Rome was on the brink of series of invasions that would crumble what had been the once great Roman Empire. When Augustine wrote his classic *The City of God* in AD 410, the motivation was the impending invasion of North Africa by the Goths. They were followed by the Vandals, another Germanic tribe, who in AD 455 were able to enter and sack Rome itself. The Lombards, who ruled Italy for almost two hundred years, followed in AD 586. Finally, the Franks, headed by Charlemagne, reconsolidated portions of the Western empire at the end of the eighth century AD into what was labeled the Holy Roman Empire, but the Roman Empire of antiquity was long gone.

> The ancient Empire, or rather its western half, was crumbling. For centuries Roman legions had been able to hold the Germanic peoples behind their borders at the Rhine and the Danube. In Great Britain, a wall separated the Romanized areas from that which was in control of the "barbarians." But now the floodgates were open. In a series of seemingly endless waves, barbarian hordes crossed the frontiers of the empire, sacked towns and cities, and finally settled in areas that had been part of the Roman Empire. There they founded their own kingdoms, many of them theoretically subject to the Empire, but in truth independent. The Western Roman Empire had come to an end.[70]

These invading hordes were pagans. As such, the church had a new challenge—to convert these new invaders and to preserve what they could of the culture around them. Out of all of this chaos, a new civilization would arise. It would be a melting pot of Greco-Roman antiquity, Christianity, and the invaders' Germanic traditions. This process took the thousand years called the Middle (or less accurately the Dark) Ages. We shall take a look at how the monastic movement played a part in this new order of things, but before that, we should return to take quick look at what was happening in the Eastern Roman Empire.

The Rise of Islam

Just about the time that things were beginning to settle down in the West with the rise of the Frankish Empire in the seventh century, something unexpected happened. Out of Arabia, an area of the world generally ignored by the Romans, came a tidal wave of conquest that threatened to engulf the known world. In a few years, the Persian Empire had disappeared, and much of what had been part of the ancient Roman Empire in the East was now in the hands of the Arabs.

The driving force behind this surge of conquest was a man named Mohammed and the religion he would found, Islam. Mohammed was an Arab merchant who had some familiarity with the Jewish and Christian religions acquired through his travels. He claimed to have received a vision from the archangel Gabriel about a one true God who was both just and demanding. He believed his visions were just the culmination of the revelation given to the Hebrew prophets and to Jesus Christ (whom he saw as a great prophet, but not divine). When his message was not well received by the polytheistic merchants of Mecca, he took refuge at the oasis at Medina that eventually became a great city. Mohammed waged a military and political campaign that eventually brought him control over Mecca and much of the Arabia.

At Mohammed's death in AD 632, leadership of this new religion passed on to a series of caliphs (Arabic for *successor*) who instituted an expansionist philosophy that saw in rapid succession the fall of

Syria, Damascus, Jerusalem, and Egypt, then the remainder of North Africa, and eventually southern Spain. They also solidified their control of the remainder of the Persian Empire. These invasions had enormous significance for Christianity. Many of the ancient centers of Christianity—Jerusalem, Antioch, Carthage, Alexandria, and Damascus—were now under Muslim rule.

Of even greater significance was the change in the geographic configuration of Christianity. Until this time, Christianity had grown around the Mediterranean Basin from east to west. Now, it would find the center along an axis that ran from north to south from the British Isles, the Frankish Kingdom, and Italy. This accelerated the division of the church in to eastern and western traditions as the popes more closely aligned themselves with the new Holy Roman Empire of the Frankish kings and ignored the historical ties with Constantinople.

With this political background, we will now take a look at medieval monasticism.

Medieval Monasticism

The first non-Roman area to establish an extensive network of monasteries were the Irish. How the Irish monastic movement originated is unclear although many scholars believe it originated with missionaries from Britain or Gaul.[71] The well know Saint Patrick, who died in AD 461, created a church structure similar to the one created in other areas of world, but the great period of monastic development followed in the sixth century. Tradition credits Saint Finnian as having the critical role in the development of the movement. He founded a small community at Clonard that blossomed into a series of monasteries throughout the country.[72]

These were coenobitical, or community-based, monasteries, although it was not uncommon for an individual monk to on occasion depart for a period of isolation in the nearby countryside. The hermitage tradition found some receptivity among the rugged and individualistic Irish, but the practice of discipline and accountability afforded in community eventually won out.

As in other monastic traditions, rules outlining behavior and governance of the community eventually developed. No Irish rule older than that of Saint Columbanus has been discovered, and this rule, along with other of his writings, gives us great insight into daily Irish monastic living. For Columbanus, the life of the monk was one in constant battle to defeat sensuality and self-will. Reflective of the harsh environment outside the walls of the monastery, the physical demands and strict discipline for even minor offenses were designed to strengthen the spirit and turn the individual monk more quickly to a path of complete dependence on and obedience to the example of Jesus Christ.

Also, in contrast to the Egyptian monks and some of those who followed, the Irish monks did not appear to have any concerns about reading the ancient Roman and Greek classics. In fact, this growing love of study and reading began to establish a base for the monastery as the hotbed of learning. By the end of the seventh century, this enthusiasm for and love of study had made the Irish monastic schools the most famous in Europe.[73] These schools were also important centers of book reproduction, and children were brought in to copy many of the manuscripts that had been salvaged from libraries decimated on the continent during the Barbarian invasions. Eventually, these copied manuscripts were then exported back to the continent to reestablish learning centers during the medieval period.

Another export from Ireland was the monastic organization of the Celtic church. The Irish monastic movement was rooted within the sociopolitical structure of Irish civilization as a whole. The strength of the clan structure and local autonomy of the clan leader led many of them to associate closely with the local monastery. In fact, many of the abbots came from the local leader's family, and many of the monasteries were located on donated land. For example, Saint Columba was also a prince of the Ui Neill, the most powerful dynasty in Northern Ireland.[74]

When Saint Columbanus immigrated to Gaul, his first missionary efforts were directed at the Merovingian nobility to ensure their support and sponsorship of his efforts. Over the next few generations, this collaboration blossomed and produced several monastic communities of both men and women. It was also at these continental monasteries that the more stringent *Rule of Saint Columbanus* was confronted by the *Rule of Saint Benedict*. Although some mixing of the *Rules* occurred, by and large the less harsh *Rule of Saint Benedict* emerged as the governing instrument of these communities.[75] As such, the monastic tradition emerging out of the early Middle Ages was one that was both more tolerant from a disciplinary perspective but also one where the idea of study and teaching gained nearly equal footing with the emphasis on prayer, meditation, obedience, and silence.

Women in Monasticism

As one would expect, men were not the only individuals captured by the idea of living holy and consecrated lives dedicated to worship and prayer to the Lord. As early as the mid fourth century we have documented examples of women leading monastic lives. Macrina (c. 327–380), the sister of Basil the Great and Saint Gregory of Nyssa (two of the three Great Cappadocian Fathers of the Eastern Christian faith), accepted a life of spiritual dedication.

The early church at times sent mixed messages to the women of the church. Although Paul had proclaimed that "There is neither male nor female, neither bond nor free; for you are all one in Christ Jesus,"[76] in general women were perceived in both Christian and non-Christian society as being intellectually and physically inferior.[77] However, no less potential critic than her own brother, Gregory of Nyssa, had this to say about his sister: "In this case it was a woman who provided us with our subject—if indeed she should be styled woman, for as I do not know whether it is fitting to designate her by her sex, who has so surpassed her sex."[78]

Despite the harshness of the environment, there is some indication that a few women did successfully live in the predominantly masculine environment of the desert hermits.[79] A more common approach was for the women to live as "house-ascetic," whereby they would exercise the spiritual disciplines of prayer, fasting, and abstinence in the confines of their own homes.[80] Eventually communal arrangements for women began to appear, often in proximity to the male monasteries, but with a requirement of strict separation due to the predominant emphasis on sexual abstinence that was a fundamental tenant of early monastic orders.

Where the leadership of the monastic orders and notable figures in the movement were primarily men, the interesting thing is that when we review the history of Christian spirituality in a later chapter, many of the most notable characters are female. This leads to the interesting speculation that while men may have ventured forth and established the concept of discipline and communal organization, it is women who may have set the best example of a life consecrated to the spiritual aspects of the faith.

The Monastic Movement Is Reformed

Although certainly not intended by Benedict, the structure of the *Rule* provided many ingredients to create a power base for the monasteries observing the *Rule*. A common set of governing principles allowed the independent monasteries to create a linked network together that was further refined as time progressed. The collection of people and property owned by the abbeys (either through direct donation by the individual monks or through donations by other parties) led to an economic power base that could not be ignored by the other elements of leadership. On more than one occasion, the monastic movement was not reluctant to exercise this power either collectively or through its individual adherents. The accumulation of such wealth and focus on earthly affairs ultimately led to the need for reform of the monastic movement itself as the monks moved away from the principles of the *Rule of Saint Benedict* and the great abbeys of Europe began to look as corrupt as the papacy had become over the centuries.

Into this void for reform emerged the Abbey of Cluny and the Cluniac reforms. Duke William established this new monastery at the turn of the tenth century, providing it with an independence that proved to be crucial. Of paramount importance was the right of each abbot to appoint his own successor. Although not in strict accordance with Benedictine Rule, this was the primary factor in the ascendancy of the Cluniac monks, as this resulted in a series of leaders who were selected based on ability rather than political connections. This environment produced Odo (926–944), Aymard (944–965), Mayeul (965–994), Odilo (994–1048), and Hugh (1049–1109), "six spiritual leaders of genius, each of whom in his own way stamped his imprint not only upon the regime of Cluny but also upon the religious life of his age."[81]

Many of the characteristics of the Cluniac ideal were the creation of Odo. To his disciples, Odo himself seemed a living embodiment of the Benedictine ideal. During Odo's regime, the monastery at Cluny gained a widespread reputation. His charismatic personality made him a noted figure throughout the continent. His reputation beyond France was demonstrated by the fact that only twenty-five years after Cluny's founding, Odo was invited by the secular ruler of Rome to come and reform the monasteries in that city.

Mayeul continued Odo's reforming ways and was often charged with visiting other monasteries and reforming them to the "Cluny way." However, it was under the regime of Odilo and Hugh that the great spiritual network of Cluny reached its zenith. The extraordinary reign of these two men, both of whom lived into old age, lasted for a hundred and fifteen years. Both were constant travelers who added monasteries to the Cluny empire, including abbeys in France, Italy, Spain, and Germany. Odilo secured from Pope John XIX complete exemption from local jurisdiction and control of local diocese by placing the monks of Cluny under the direct authority of the Holy See. Since the leadership of Cluny was a major influence on the selection of the popes during this time, as a practical matter Cluny communities became an almost autonomous power unto themselves.[82] With this power base the learned abbots of Cluny were the prominent counselors at the courts of popes and emperors and were arguably the ecclesiastical and political power base for most of the Western church during the eleventh and twelfth centuries. This was certainly a far cry from the monastic ideal of Saint Antony when he first wandered into the desert to seek separation from this earthly world. Eventually, this accumulation of wealth and power also served to diminish the spiritual effectiveness of the Cluniac movement. Just as they had begun as a reform movement two hundred years earlier, the ease of life enjoyed by the Clunics led to counterreformations.

The most prominent figure of the second wave of monastic reforms was Bernard of Clairvaux. At the age of twenty-three (in 1112), Bernard presented himself to the monastery of Citeaux. Bernard was a charismatic figure whose avowed purpose was to return the monastic movement to a strict observance of the *Rule of Saint Benedict.* Under his rule, the Cistercian Order (as the monks of Citeaux were called) returned with zeal to the simplistic lifestyle they envisioned Benedict had in mind.

This zeal applied to everything—dress, food, buildings, and furniture. In contrast to the linen underwear and black habit of the Benedictine monks, the Cistercians adopted a coarse habit of undyed sheep's wool. The Cistercians developed their own architectural idiom of simple rectangular structure with no towers and a plain façade. Even the sights selected for the monasteries were more remote to preserve seclusion and promote isolation from the rest of the world.[83]

Bernard also restored the facet of monastic life that prescribed manual labor. Cistercian writers stressed the value of work as an ascetical exercise as well as a means of producing food. The Cistercians did more than labor. They maintained much of the liturgical tradition of the Benedictine way. Although they did drop many of the Cluniac ceremonies, there was still the divine office to sing, daily masses to be said, and time for private meditation and study.[84]

Despite Bernard's desire to stay focused on the world to come, his gift for oratory and his desire to see the ecclesiastical structure of the day reformed did ultimately lead him to be an arbitrator in many political and ecclesiastical disputes. "His personality dominated his time, for he was at once the mystic devoted to the contemplation of the humanity of Christ, the power behind and above the papacy, the champion of ecclesiastical reform, the preacher of the Second Crusade, and the enemy of all theological innovation."[85] As such, Bernard and the Cistercian movement came to impact all of Western society, much as the Cluniac movement had done over a century earlier.

A New Kind of Knighthood

Of all the new forms of the monastic life that emerged from the religious ferment of the twelfth century, none was more original or more seemingly paradoxical than that of the military orders. These were orders of knights, dedicated to fighting the infidels, who were also professing monks.[86] To some extent these knight monks appear a contradiction in terms. How can fighting and killing be reconciled to Christ's message of peace and love? The reconciliation of these two diverse occupations in the same individual can only be understood in the context of the crusading movement from which they originated.

The change in attitude toward physical violence can be tied back to the emergence of the new ideal of Christian knighthood. By the Cluniacs and others, the soldiers of the day were encouraged to adopt certain codes of conduct, and the concept of "just war" was further refined. Eventually, the idea of killing an infidel in battle evolved from a sin to a meritorious act, which even served to remit temporal punishment due for sin. [87]

The two major orders were the Order of Hospitallers and the Knight of the Temple. The later were called in to existence when Jerusalem was opened to religious pilgrimages in the early part of the twelfth century. "Holy warriors" of some type were needed to patrol the routes from brigands and Muslim raiders. Started by the knight Hugh de Payns, the group took vows of chastity and obedience, followed some form of communal life, and partook in some type of divine office. The order received papal approval in 1129, and the ranks soon swelled with recruits eager to perform service for the Lord with sword as well as song.[88]

The Hospitallers had a more traditional origin in that they were originally organized as a fraternity to serve and care for the poor and sick pilgrims to Jerusalem. Inspired by the Knight of the Temple, they began to provide military protection against invasions from Muslim invaders. They too followed the example of the Knights and participated in vespers, lived communal lives, and followed personal vows of poverty and chastity.

The military orders had been born out of the first Crusades during the period of partial occupancy by the West of the Holy Lands. As succeeding crusades proved ever more fruitless, the relevancy of the Orders began to be questioned. Eventually the Hospitallers returned to their origins as maintainers and staffers of hospitals. The Templars suffered a less happy fate. Eventually, the accumulation of wealth of the Templars proved too tempting for King Philip IV of France, who accused the order of heresy, extracted false confession under torture, and then executed the majority of the order. The weak Pope Clement V did nothing to protect the order, and they were ordered to disband on March 22, 1312.[89]

The Friars of the Mendicant Orders

At the beginning of the thirteenth century, the monastic movement underwent yet another radical revival in an attempt to reform itself from the monastic traditions of the past. These new orders were called Mendicants, because they earned their living by begging.

> But their rejection of the property and reliance upon begging to support themselves was only the outward sign of a more fundamental change of spirit. The mendicant Orders broke free from one of the most basic principles of traditional monasticism by abandoning the seclusion and enclosure of the cloister in order to engage in an active pastoral mission to the society of their time.[90]

As can be seen from the review of other reform movements, this is truly a radical departure. Time and again, the accumulation of corporate wealth at the monastic orders had eventually led to the erosion of the spirituality of the group. In addition, accumulation of wealth and property had led to the leadership of these orders to often act more like secular-world power brokers instead of humble servants of the Lord. The social context out of which the Mendicants evolved can best be exemplified by examining the leading proponent of the movement: Francis of Assisi.

Francis was born into a well-to-do bourgeois family. As a youth, he aspired to the position of knighthood, and with this view, he set out in the spring of 1205 to join the military to expel the German imperial power from southern Italy. On the way to enlist, he had a vision that told him he was not suited for the military life and returned home. As a young man he was captivated by the hermitical ideal and left the comforts of home to live a solitary life in caves and ruined churches. Before long he acquired a group of followers from the small town of Assisi. Instead of continuing the life of a hermit, Francis decided to live the life of an itinerant preacher. He was deeply impacted one day when he heard a message preached from Matthew 10 admonishing him to "preach as you go.... Take no gold or silver; for a laborer is worthy of his pay." With this ideal, he advocated an absolute poverty beyond that of prior orders. To Francis this became the literal imitation of the earthly life of Christ.[91] Francis drew many followers, and his little friars begging, singing, and preaching throughout Europe became a common sight.

The founder of the other major mendicant order was Saint Dominic. A contemporary of Francis, his order of preachers grew out of Dominic's involvement in preaching against the heresy of the Cathars. As such, from the start, it was a clerical and learned order that put great emphasis on study. Soon, the Dominicans were present at the major theological universities, and such Dominicans as Albert the Great and Thomas Aquinas would begin to establish the order as a producer of the leading minds of the late Middle Ages.

This love of knowledge and study made the universities and monasteries run by the monks a hotbed of learning, discussion, and debate. Out of this environment arose monks who challenged the thought of the Catholic Church at that time. Most recognizable among those was the Augustinian monk Martin Luther.

Post-Reformation

Most well-read evangelicals are familiar with the key points of the Reformation. The decay of the Catholic Church led to a deadened faith that placed the church hierarchy in a position greater than biblical authority. In addition, the path to salvation for the lay parishioner was road blocked with a works-based system that made a mockery of the finality of the substitutionary death of Christ on the cross and victory over sin based on faith alone. However, this did not open the door for a faith where spirituality and heavenly focus no longer had a place in the believer's daily life. On the contrary, the Reformation should have opened up the laypeople to realize that they individually were capable of having a direct and deep relationship with God themselves. This in fact did happen within many of the Protestant denominations, and pietism had a rebirth of sorts.

Ironically, the Protestant Reformation triggered within the Roman Catholic Church a counterreformation that rejuvenated both the church and the monastic movement as well.

> Although it is true that monastic life had reached a low ebb at the outset of the Reformation, it is also true that there were still many in convents and monasteries who took their vows seriously, and who bemoaned the sad state of monastic life. During the sixteenth century, such longings came to fruition in the reformation of the old orders and in the founding of new ones. Among these new orders, some sought to renew the ancient strict observance of monastic vows, whereas others were shaped

to respond to the new conditions of the sixteenth century. The most noteworthy new order of the first type was that of the Discalced Carmelites, founded by St. Teresa. The Jesuits, under the leadership of Ignatius Loyola, were foremost among the orders that hoped to respond to the new times with new solutions.[92]

We shall hear more of the story of Saint Teresa of Avila in the next chapter on Christian spirituality and return to Saint Ignatius Loyola when we examine spiritual exercises and practices in chapter six.

Summary

One can see the widespread impact the multifaceted aspects of these groups of men and women had on both our Christian faith and culture at large. Starting from the early desert fathers and their desire to escape from this world via a radical focus on Christ, through the medieval orders whose powers rivaled that of kings and popes, to the simplistic lifestyle of the Mendicants who valued preaching and teaching, one can see both the best (and potentially worst) of living a life radically focused on one's faith. Without a doubt, there is much to be admired about the various facets of the monastic life. A focus on the disciplines of prayer, meditation, study, contemplation, fasting, and service should be encouraged in every Christian's life. While pursuing these to the extremes of some of the monks is not healthy, the total de-emphasis of these traditional spiritual disciplines in the contemporary Christians life is certainly regrettable. The strong commitment to Christian community in contrast to the emphasis of modern society on the individual at all cost should certainly be a call back to Christian fellowship. The desire to model Christ to an unbelieving world through total reliance on the provision of our daily need should be a wakeup call to the modern world of materialism.

In contrast, though, one should also recognize that even though the intention of the monastic order was admirable, there are certainly lessons to be learned from the negative side of the movement. Multiple times the orders succumbed to the accumulation of wealth that lead to the involvement with the secular world in a form not honoring of God. The involvement with the orders in the Crusades evidenced a lack of understanding of Christ's command for peace.

Probably the most critical fault of the monastic movement is the total division of the sacred and secular. Following in the Platonic tradition that involvement in earthly affairs was inherently a second-rate activity, the monastic movement aided in the further division of those involved in a religious vocation from the common man that reached its apex in the Middle Ages. This separation would be one of the major areas that reformers would attack.

> Rejecting monasticism, they (the reformers) preached that the Christian life is not a summons to a state of life separate from our participation in the creation order of family and work, but is embedded with the creation order ... and in the concept of the priesthood of all believers.[93]

Yet in balance, one can appreciate the heritage that every Christian has in the monastic movement. These men and women set standards of love and devotion to the Trinity that are a challenge to a culture that all too often is self-centered and superficial. They are an encouragement to the modern Christian hoping to change that culture.

This spirit of focused time in prayer and practice of the spiritual disciplines is an example that still has merit in today's society. This growth in spiritual formation is never more needed than in a world that is clearly post-Christian in culture. The impact of even a small group of people who set an example of spirituality that is evident to even the most callous of the world can speak volumes where all the preaching in the world will have no impact. We will next take a look at a few of those individuals who practiced a Christian spirituality that set them apart and figuratively made them saints on earth.

Chapter 5: Christian Spirituality

What practicing Christian would not want to lead a deep and abiding life resting comfortably in the knowledge that he or she has a personal and intimate relationship with the Lord of the universe? Yet like all good things, many of us, despite our best intentions, find it immensely difficult (if not impossible) to lead such a life. Yet throughout the history of Christianity, there have been men and women who we might view as extraordinary (even though they would not) in the intensity and intimacy of their relationship with all three persons of the Trinity. It would seem appropriate to spend a few pages reviewing the story of Christian spirituality and the lessons it teaches for the "average" Christian, even today.

Before we begin to examine the lives of those who exhibited true Christian spirituality it would be helpful to define what is meant by the term. The root word *spirit* comes from the Latin word *spiritus*, whose primary meaning is *breath*. This brings to mind something that is physical but also invisible, such as the air we breathe. The word *spirit* then came to mean those invisible qualities that shape a person's life, such as love, truth, peace, and courage. It is the sum of those real but invisible qualities that make us who we in essence are.[94]

Adding the word *Christian* to the word *spirituality* clarifies that we are reviewing those distinctive characteristics of the Christian faith that truly make us followers of Jesus Christ. As such, when one is exhibiting Christian spirituality, one leads all of life, both physical and spiritual, from the perspective of their relationship with God the Father through Jesus Christ. Someone who is noted for their Christian spirituality is someone who is recognized by others for leading a life that seeks to imitate the life of Christ—a life characterized by an intense focus on their relationship with their Creator and a life characterized by devotion and obedience to the Word of God (which is, after all, "God breathed").[95] This individual manages to keep an eternal perspective when all of those around him or her seem to be lost.

Of course, the story of Christian spirituality must begin with the story of Jesus Christ, His life and teaching and death and resurrection and the impact this had on his followers. But it is also the story of the Holy Spirit. The indwelling of the Holy Spirit in followers of Christ will enable them to be more Christlike. He is the "helper" promised by Jesus in John 14:16. In addition, God the Father is the focus of our adoration. All three persons of the Trinity are involved when we seek to deepen our faith and live lives that are clear examples of our faith and the hope that is in us. Over the centuries, there have been men and women who have been able to capture some of this desire on paper and through the lives they led. Let us take a look at some of these individuals and the spiritual classics they penned.

Revelations of Divine Love and Julian of Norwich

Julian of Norwich (1342–1417) was a Benedictine nun who was not widely known during her lifetime but has become widely esteemed in more recent times. She spent most of her adult life as an anchoress. As an anchoress, she voluntarily confined herself to a cell constructed adjacent to a church. As such, she was able to withdraw from the world and become anchored to the church. However, even under such an arrangement, she was not totally isolated. As people attended the church, they would often visit with her through an opening in the wall and seek her counsel and advice. Her reputation for wisdom and holiness grew throughout that section of England, and she was visited regularly by the poor and noble alike.

When Julian was a young woman, she suffered from illness that more than once brought her to the brink of death. During this illness, she experienced visions that she called "showings." She wrote down what she had been shown and later added to these writings with further analysis and other thoughts. These were eventually published under the title *Revelations of Divine Love,* which is thought to be the first book ever published in the English language by a woman.[96]

However, even though the earliest edition dates back to 1670, when it was released under the editing of Benedictine Serenus Cressy, it remained little noticed until the 1901 version edited by Grace Warrack was released. Due to Warrack's careful editing and more sympathetic introduction, the book became a popular source for lectures and discussions due to some of its more novel theological views. The subsequent annotated version of Julian's works released in 1979 has become a staple of those studying the woman who has become widely recognized as one of Britain's most important mystics.

Julian herself wrote in the plain vernacular of the common people. She believed that the revelations given to her were not private, but should be available to followers of Christ at large. Theologically, some of her writings are controversial, as they hint at an almost universal salvation. However, she was often quick to point out that God had only revealed to her the fate of the redeemed, not of the damned.[97]

Julian grew up during a time of great turmoil. Plagues were ravaging the land. Although very little is known about her early life, there has been some speculation that she may have been a widow who lost both husband and child to illness before becoming a nun. Regardless of her personal background, what made Julian's theology stand out was her constant focus on God as a God of mercy and love versus one of rules and discipline. Even times of personal suffering were not times of punishment for sin (as was widely taught at the time) but rather of opportunity to refocus our lives around Jesus Christ as the Savior. The pain and suffering we endure in this world can serve to purify us, to teach us, and to make us more reliant on God.

She found in the passion of Christ the key to understanding all that was evil in the world. Creation and redemption are united together in those who recognized salvation in Jesus Christ. She famously wrote, "It is true that sin is the cause of all this pain; but all shall be well, and all shall be well, and all manner of things shall be well…. Of all the pains that led to salvation, this is the greatest, to see your love suffer. How could any pain be more to me than to see the one who is all my life, my bliss, my joy, suffer?"[98]

Julian also described God as both a mother and a father. In her discussion of the Trinity, she described Jesus as portraying the motherly attributes of being wise and loving. Theologians are split as to whether Julian meant this in the metaphorical way or really viewed Christ as the divine mother. There is no doubt she held the relationship between mother and child as the greatest in human terms and the closest comparison of the potential relationship between God and His human creation.[99] It is for this last view that Julian has been identified with the feminist theology movement.

Julian's book has become a spiritual classic due to both its content and its readability. Her aim was for everyone to be able to enjoy it. It is divided into numerous short chapters, making it easy to break into segments for reflective reading on a periodic basis. Her message is one of both peace and hope. God is good, He is in charge, He loves his people, and in turn His people are safe with God, even in times of temporal trials and tribulations. Thomas Merton wrote, "The theology of Julian of Norwich is a theology of mercy, of joy, and of praise. Nowhere in all of Christian literature are the dimensions of her Christian optimism excelled."[100]

The Imitation of Christ and Thomas à Kempis

Unlike Julian of Norwich, Thomas à Kempis was widely read and very influential during his lifetime. In particular, his book *The Imitation of Christ* was recognized early on as a spiritual classic and quoted often in the pulpits of churches in his native Germany and remained so even after the Reformation some hundred years later.[101]

Thomas was born in Kempin, Germany, in 1379. "À Kempis" literally means "of Kempin," his birth town. His surname was actually Hemerken (or "little hammer") in his native tongue. Appropriately enough, his father was a blacksmith and his mother was a schoolteacher. As a nineteen-year-old, he followed his older brother to Mount Saint Agnes monastery, about seventy-five miles from his birthplace, and remained there until his death over seventy-two years later at age ninety-two.

In 1429 he was appointed subprior of the monastery. One of his responsibilities was that of novice master. In this role, he was responsible for instructing those new to the community and to spiritual life. It was to those novitiates and others like them that *The Imitation of Christ* was addressed.

Kempis's ministry was part of the New Devotion movement founded by Gerard Groote. Members called themselves the Brothers and Sisters of the Common Life and were less concerned about theology and doctrinal issues and much more focused on fostering an intimate relationship with God.[102]

As you would guess from the title, *The Imitation of Christ* it instructs the reader on how to grow spiritually by following the example of Christ in both general terms and interior attitudes and through partaking in Holy Communion. It is full of common-sense advice that advocates humbleness and contrition and emphasizes piety over doctrine. The piety reflected is more focused on individual piety than the piety of the community.[103]

For the author, a certain amount of withdrawal from the outside world was necessary to grow spiritually. Thomas à Kempis only ventured outside the walls of his monastery on two occasions during the last fifty years of his life. With his singular focus on leading the spiritual life, his attitude was one of contemplation, and he would likely have only viewed the outside world as a distraction from that pursuit. However, he did place some emphasis on taking care of ourselves physically so that we might be better able to serve God's purpose for us in the world.[104] In book one, chapter three, he wrote, "At the Day of Judgment we will not be asked what we have read, but what we have done."

For some five hundred years, *The Imitation of Christ* has been considered the consummate spiritual classic. It has been published in thousands of editions and literally read by millions. Many church historians consider it second only to the Bible in readership and impact. Partly attributable to its success is the readability of the work. It is filled with pithy sayings that are both memorable and insightful.

In recent times it has fallen off somewhat in popularity. It is criticized more for what it doesn't say than what it does. The heavy emphasis on withdrawal from the world and lack of appreciation for study in addition to meditation seems a little out of touch with the emphasis on activity in today's church. However, *The Imitation of Christ* is meant primarily as an encouragement to leading a deeper spiritual life—one for which Jesus Christ has set an example. There can be little argument that this is a relevant and worthy goal for any sincere Christian.

The Practice of the Presence of God and Brother Lawrence

Brother Lawrence was born Nicholas Herman in a small village in the French region of Lorraine. His exact date of birth is in dispute, with dates ranging from late 1611 to early 1614. The fact that his birthdate is not even known with any certainty may lead one to believe he was not particularly well known by his contemporaries, and that would be correct. However, his relative obscurity during his lifetime and the humbleness of his life make Brother Lawrence an ideal example of how a life well lived by an ordinary man can provide profound insights into everyday spirituality.

As a young man, he grew up in poverty and was eventually compelled to join the French army to guarantee some level of daily sustenance. During this period of army service, he had a conversion experience. While gazing upon a barren tree in wintertime, he was struck by how much his soul was like that tree—it was barren of any fruit or leaves. However, just as the tree would be transformed by the coming of the spring and burst forth into new life, so too would his soul be renewed by the coming of the Holy Spirit, and he could look forward to evidencing the fruit of the Spirit if he accepted God. From that moment forth, he never seemed to lose his singular focus on loving and obeying God.

Shortly after this experience, he was wounded in battle and was discharged upon his recovery. Seeking to honor this newfound love, he entered the Discalced Carmelite monastery in Paris as a lay brother. His primary responsibility was to be in charge of the kitchen. Amidst all the mundane tasks and bidding of his superiors, he developed his own rules of spirituality and work. Key to his attitude was that no matter how routine the work being done was, it would serve as a medium for conveying God's love. In effect, not only was it a spiritually focused activity that could honor God, but in fact, even when washing the dishes, one could also do the task for the honor of God and service to others.

Over his years of service he became known as a friendly and loving person who exhibited an extraordinary spirituality. In 1666–67 he was interviewed about his spirituality by Joseph de Beaufort, counsel to the Paris archbishop. Shortly after Brother Lawrence's death in February 1691, de Beaufort published the interviews along with some biographical information and "spiritual maxims" in a book that he titled *The Practice of the Presence of God*.[105]
As the name would suggest, Brother Lawrence advocates continual prayer and awareness of God's presence all around us until the awareness becomes a matter of habit.

> The time of action does not differ from that of prayer. I possess God as peacefully in the bustle of my kitchen, where sometimes several people are asking me for different things at the same time, as I do upon my knees before the Blessed Sacrament. This practice of the presence of God must stem from the heart, from love rather than from the understanding and speech. In the way of God, thought counts for little. Love does everything and it is not needful to have great things to

do. I turn my little omelet in the pan for the love of God. When it is finished, if I have nothing to do, I prostrate myself on the ground and worship my God, who gave me the grace to make it after which I arise happier than a king. People look for ways of learning how to love God. They hope I attain it by I know not how many different practices … Is it not a shorter and more direct way to do everything for the love of God, to make use of all the tasks one's lot in life demands to show him that love, and to maintain his presence within by the communion of our heart with his? There is nothing complicated about it. One has only to turn to it honestly and simply.[106]

To Brother Lawrence, the key to leading a life that was most Christlike was to lead a life of spontaneous prayer. He described being frustrated with formulaic prayers and fixed prayer times and advocated instead a life of heartfelt prayer that is both spontaneous and sincere. To aid in this attitude, he advocated conversational prayer in everyday vernacular. The heart of his message is that it is not so much what we do, but why we do it.[107]

While many Christians today would view this state of constant connectivity to God as unrealistic, Brother Lawrence would argue that anyone is capable of "prayer without ceasing."[108] He also advised that a life of simplicity that avoided the trivialities and distractions of life would accelerate one's growth toward spiritual maturity. Yet he would also acknowledge that we are all still fallen and prone to sin, but instead of feeling discouraged, we should just confess our sins, seek God's pardon, and move on with a renewed conviction to learn from our mistakes and seek God's presence with even more fervor.

It is for this sincere and practical type of advice that Brother Lawrence and his writings have remained in print all of these centuries and given comfort to so many Christians who are seeking to make God more real and present in their daily lives.

The Serious Call to a Devout and Holy Life and William Law

William Law was born in 1686 in Northamptonshire, England. In 1705 he entered Emmanuel College at Cambridge, where he excelled as a student. In 1711 he was named a fellow and was ordained. For the next few years he taught at the school, but in 1714 George I became king, ending the reign of the Stuarts, and Law, who had already expressed Jacobite tendencies, was dismissed from his position for refusing to take the oath of allegiance to the new government.

Law was taken in by Edward Gibbon, ostensibly as a tutor for his son, whose name was Edward as well. (Not to be too confusing, but it was Edward Senior's grandson, Edward Junior's son, Edward Gibbon III who was the noted historian who wrote the multivolume set *The Rise and Fall of the Roman Empire.*) Law held this position for ten years and over that time became not only a tutor but also a spiritual counselor to the Gibbon family and many of their visiting friends. In fact, many of the religious luminaries of that time credit Law for having a profound impact on their way of viewing what it meant to live a devout Christian life. Among the more recognizable names were John and Charles Wesley, William Wilberforce, and George Whitfield.

Edward Senior died in 1736, and the household dispersed in 1737. In 1740 Law was able to retire to Kings Cliffe, a house with some property he had inherited from his father. It was there, with a couple of his followers, that he attempted to lead the type of reflective and spiritual life he wrote and talked about for the remaining twenty-one years of his life until his death in 1761.[109]

Early in his life, when he was only twenty-one years old, Law defined for himself certain principles for living his life that he captured in the his "Rules for My Future Conduct" several which are captured below[110]:

I.   To fix it deep in my mind that I have but one business upon my hands—to seek for eternal happiness by doing the will of God.

II.   To examine everything that relates to me in this view, as it serves or obstructs this only end of life.

III. To think nothing great or desirable because the world thinks it so, but to form all my judgments of things from the infallible word of God, and direct my life according to it.

IV.   To avoid all concerns with the world, or the ways of it, except where religion requires.

V.   To remember frequently, and impress it upon my mind deeply, that no condition of this life is for enjoyment, but for trial.

VI.   That the greatness of human nature consists of nothing else but in imitating the divine nature …

VII. To spend as little time as I possibly can among such persons as can receive no benefit from me nor me from them.

VIII. To be always fearful of letting my time slip away without some fruit …

IX.   To think humbly of myself, and with great charity of all others …

X.   To spend some time in giving an account of the day, previous to evening prayer. How have I spent the day? What sin have I committed? What temptation have I withstood? Have I performed all my duty?

Although Law wrote several books and treatises over his lifetime, the one that has had the most lasting impact was the 1729 volume he titled *The Serious Call to a Devout and Holy Life*. Law began by defining *devotion* as a life given over (devoted) to God. He further encouraged readers that not just our prayer life but also every aspect and action we undertake should be a focal point for bringing honor to God. After all, he reasoned, if our daily actions do not demonstrate the guiding power of the Holy Spirit, how can we call ourselves Christians? To Law, to pray and go to church without leading a holy life outside of the church was extremely hypocritical and should call someone's true nature as a being reconciled to God through Jesus into question. The Christian lifestyle is exemplified by renouncing wealth, idleness, and folly and cultivating humility and self-denial. Law recognized that we cannot be perfected in this world, but we all can surely do better than we are now. For Law, the Sermon on the Mount contains the admonitions that we should follow if we seek to be true followers of Christ.

Law then gave descriptions of how to and not to live lives of singular focus on the will of God. He drew verbal portraits of typical characters and personalities found in God's kingdom on earth. Miranda (wonderful), Classicus (classical), Flavis (extravagant), Calidus (wasteful), Eusebia (reverent), Succus (disheartened), Mundanus (worldly), and Flatus are all as recognizable today as they were when Law wrote about them nearly three hundred years ago. A few are truly good and a few are truly evil, but most of the characters attempt to lead lives of compromise between God's will for us and the spirit of the age.[111] In this state of compromise, no one can be truly at peace. We have this nagging feeling of uneasiness that can only be eliminated once we fully dedicate ourselves to following our Lord.

Law's admonition about the use and misuse of our money and our time are key themes throughout the book. For example, he gave us Calidus, who is so busy working that he feels he cannot make time for prayer or to slow down and observe the world around him. He is motivated to make money to provide luxuries for his family so that one day they can find time to relax and enjoy their treasures. Every reader can quickly associate this individual with someone in the realm of his or her own personal experience. This timeless connectivity is what makes a read of *A Serious Call to a Devout and Holy Life* as profitable today as it was to the readers of the eighteenth century.

Evelyn Underhill's Defining Mysticism

We leap forward a couple of hundred years to take a look at the last of the writers of spiritual classics to be covered in this book. Few women of the twentieth century have done more to further our understanding of the devotional life than Evelyn Underhill.[112] Her writing and research in the areas of religion and spirituality have answered questions for skeptics and believers alike. It is from one of her quotes regarding the benefit of retreat that the title of this book comes from.

Evelyn was born in Woverhampton, England, on December 6, 1875. She grew up as the only child of a well-to-do family. Her father was a lawyer, and the family led a life that was both intellectually challenging and relatively free of any apparent stress, although neither of her parents evidently shared in her interest in spiritual matters. At an early age she incurred a longing for an understanding of the mystical world. She described these moments as "abrupt experiences of the peaceful, undifferentiated plan of reality."[113] Her attempt to explain these moments led her to a lifelong desire to research and write on matters of the spiritual.

At the age of thirty-two she married Hubert Stewart Moore whom she had grown up with and known most of her life. Moore was a lawyer and practiced law as well as wrote and taught about legal subjects. The couple never had any children, and this left Evelyn with both the resources and time to travel extensively throughout Europe, visiting churches, monasteries, and other religious sites.

Evelyn (or Mrs. Moore, as her friends would call her) was a prolific author and published over thirty manuscripts using her maiden name or, on occasion, the pseudonym "John Cordelier." Although initially an agnostic looking for answers, she grew more and more interested in the Catholic Church and eventually adopted a theological view that can best be described as Anglo-Catholic. In her transition from a theist to a Christian, she was aided by Baron Friedrich von Hugel, whom she described as her spiritual mentor. After his death in 1925, her writings began to focus much more on the power of the Holy Spirit to act in one's life to effect change both inwardly and outwardly. She began to lecture at churches and retreat centers and within a short time became a prominent spokesperson for the Anglican Church. She was in demand as a lay leader of spiritual retreats as well as a guest speaker, radio lecturer, and vocal proponent of contemplative prayer.

Underhill was educated at home, although she did attend Kings College of London, where she studied history and botany. She was conferred an honorary doctorate from Aberdeen University and was made a fellow of Kings College. She was the first woman to lecture to the clergy in the Church of England as well as the first woman to officially conduct spiritual retreats for the church. Evelyn was well schooled in the classics as well as in theology, philosophy, psychology, and physics, and this background allowed her to be nominated to the post of editor for *The Spectator,* a widely respected conservative weekly magazine that has been in continuous publication since 1828. It was this natural intellectual curiosity that led her to read and research extensively and then to assume the role of author.

Underhill's initial literary efforts were in the fiction area. She published three novels between 1904 and 1909, although even her works of fiction contained strong elements of the mystical. Her characters were often caught between two worlds, just as the Christian often finds him- or herself balancing between competing value systems. By 1911 Evelyn was ready to tackle head-on her desire to explore the spiritual nature of man, and her first effort has been deemed by most critics to be her best work—*Mysticism: A Study of the Nature and Development of Man's Spiritual Consciousness.*

Although the title of the book has a very academic sound to it, Evelyn tackles the topic in a very subjective way. In particular she sets forth that (1) mysticism is a very practical activity that is essential to the growth of the spiritual side of a person, (2) mysticism is above all a spiritual activity, (3) the love of God is the driver of all true mystical experiences, and (4) although mysticism is not a purely psychological experience, there is definitely a measurable psychological result.

She divided the book into two major parts. The first section is an introduction to the topic of mysticism, and the second a detailed analysis of the development of the human consciousness. A detailed analysis of the book would be difficult to accomplish in a few paragraphs. It is sufficient for this discussion to say that Evelyn made the first attempt to reconcile the highly spiritual aspects of the desire innate in our created self to experience in a more firsthand way the reality of our eternal nature to the emerging scientific analysis of our human psyche. She provided an explanation for the church's relevance in a culture that was quickly relegating it to an archaic tradition viewed as less relevant to a world where everything could be explained through psychoanalysis. Underhill concluded the book by reviewing the historical backgrounds of a variety of mystics and their role as vanguards in cultural understanding and pointing out the continued relevance of studying the mystics of the past as an indication of the timeless nature of creating true relationship with God our Creator.

Summary

The above books and individuals were selected from hundreds of potential candidates for discussion. That is not to suggest that all of the thoughts presented by these select authors are to be accepted carte blanche. What was meant to be dispelled was the idea that only truly uniquely gifted individuals are capable of leading lives of dedication to the Lord. Although all of the people discussed demonstrated a strong love for God, they came from a variety of backgrounds and experiences. None would have ever thought of themselves as having skills beyond those of their contemporaries. We may not want to (nor should we) be isolated in a small room attached to our local church as Julian of Norwich was. However, we should want to have the desire to grow in our spiritual maturity and become more singularly focused on leading lives that honor to God.

After reading the last three chapters that have looked at the historical growth of the contemplative life of the monks and spiritualists over the last 1,900 years, notice how often the concept of prayer entered into this growth in spiritual maturity. In the next chapter we will look at how prayer and other spiritual disciplines that have been practiced over the years aid an individual in this movement to become more Christlike. We will also explore why these disciplines can have the same effect on Christians today.

Chapter 6: The Spiritual Disciplines

As we review the lives of those who have come before us that have exhibited a singular focus on doing God's will in His world, a pattern of behavior begins to develop. We see individuals who are constantly aware of God in their lives and in every task that they do. We see individuals who spent large amounts of time in prayer and reflection. We see lives that practiced physical, emotional, mental, and spiritual disciplines that aided them in creating and maintaining this intense focus on their Lord and Savior. We see individuals who viewed their lives in this world as paths of forward progress to a more desired intimacy with Jesus Christ. When we begin to see a pattern of habits and practices that are consistent among a group of people who are exhibiting desired behavior, there certainly is value in delving into what those common behaviors were to see if practicing those behaviors would in fact benefit us in our spiritual journey.

It is important to remember that as with any area of life—sports, business, or parenthood, for example—none of us are born with a mature set of these skills. We may have had an aptitude or a God-given talent, but failure to work and practice and improve these skill sets will leave us performing at a suboptimal level. So it is with leading a mature spiritual life. In this chapter we will take a look at those practices or spiritual disciplines that over the centuries people have found most helpful in moving them forward on their spiritual journey and their continued relevance to us today.

Prayer

Among all the potential disciplines, prayer stands out as the most universal of all. William Carey, a seventeenth-century Baptist missionary wrote, "Prayer—secret, fervent, believing prayer—lies at the root of all personal godliness."[114] Martin Luther stated, "I have so much business I cannot get on without spending three hours daily in prayer."[115] We also have numerous examples of the value of prayer in the Bible. Prayer or some derivation of it is used in the Bible 526 times. Jesus himself is recorded as having prayed or admonished his followers to pray forty times in the Gospels.[116] In fact, of all the spiritual disciplines, prayer is very likely the most practiced among Christians today. Think of the daily routine exercised by most professing Christians. We pray at meals, pray with our children before bed time, pray with our small group, pray individually, pray corporately in church, and pray before most major and many minor decisions in our lives. Yet for all this activity, for many, their prayer life is still a far cry from that evidenced by many of the giants of our faith and certainly the example we are given by Jesus in the Bible.

Many of us can become discouraged when we see such examples of lives singularly focused on prayer. For such individuals, prayer was not an occasional practice but was in fact the lifeblood of their daily walk in faith. But just as we cannot expect to run a marathon without months and years of preparation, we should not expect to have this deep and heartfelt prayer life without undergoing a period of development under the guidance of the Holy Spirit.

As mentioned, the Bible gives us guidance on how to pray. Given that this is only an introduction to the topic of prayer, we will be reviewing only a few selections of what God's Word has to say about communicating with Him through prayer. But this will hopefully give the average reader the foundation needed to begin the journey to a more fruitful and fulfilling prayer life.

The quintessential passage on prayer is contained as a part of Jesus' first discourse in the gospel of Matthew. Specifically he says in Matthew 6:5–15,

And when you pray, you must not be like the hypocrites. For they love to stand and pray in the synagogues and at the street corners, that they may be seen by others. Truly, I say to you, they have received their reward. But when you pray, go into your room and shut the door and pray to your Father who is in secret. And your Father who sees in secret will reward you.

And when you pray, do not heap up empty phrases as the Gentiles do, for they think that they will be heard for their many words. Do not be like them, for your Father knows what you need before you ask him. Pray then like this:

Our Father in heaven, hallowed be your name.

Your kingdom come, your will be done on earth as it is in heaven.

Give us this day our daily bread and forgive our debts as we have forgiven our debtors.

And lead us not into temptation, but deliver us from evil.

For if you forgive others their trespasses, your heavenly Father will also forgive you, but if you do not forgive others their trespasses, neither will your Father forgive your trespasses.

Contained in just these few sentences are thoughts on prayer that are truly radical when compared to how most Christian's view as the "correct way" to pray.

First, prayer is by and large an individual activity. Although other passages in the Bible advise us not to forsake gathering as a group and taking that opportunity to participate in corporate prayer, where we will really develop as prayer warriors is in the individual setting where the only participants are God and ourselves. As Jesus indicates, too often corporate prayer can devolve into an exercise where those that believe themselves the most eloquent (or the boldest) will speak out first and most frequently. Whether meaning to or not, this creates an environment where the remainder of the body often gets caught up as passive listeners focusing on what is being said instead of focusing on whom it is being said to. There is also the temptation to forget that we are praying to an audience of one, and we can wind up praying to impress those around us. This individualized approach to prayer accompanies another discipline we will look at later in this chapter—that of solitude.

Second, we should avoid using unnatural wording or phrases when we pray. God does not award style points. He is only concerned about the motivation of our prayers. In fact, being overly concerned about following a particular formula for prayer can make us like the Gentiles Jesus described. We are long on content but short on depth and sincerity.

What is prayer at its heart? It is a conversation with God. Granted, talking with an omnipotent, omniscient, omnipresent, ethereal being can be pretty intimidating. However, He is God our Father, and we should remember that He created and loves us like we love our children. As such, we should feel comfortable carrying on a conversation with Him, and we should use conversational language.

Most importantly, as in any conversation, gaps should be left in the discussion to allow God to respond to us. If you had the opportunity to sit down in a one-on-one conversation with your favorite professional athlete or the president of the United States, you would not rush through the time together. You would not talk about yourself and then as soon as you were done talking end the conversation and walk away. This is the Creator of the universe. Certainly don't spend all your time telling Him what in fact He already knows (remember the characteristic of omniscience).

Third, our initial focus when we pray should be on praising God and acknowledging His lordship over all of creation. Again, you wouldn't meet the president of the United States and not at least acknowledge your gratitude for his meeting with you. How much more should you recognize the privilege we have to talk with God Almighty?

Fourth, we should not be reluctant to ask God to intercede for us, but this intercession should not only occur when we have a major crisis in our lives. Asking God to "give us our daily bread" serves to emphasize that in all things we are dependent on God's grace in our lives. Too many individuals only get sincere in their prayer life when they think that the situation is beyond their ability to handle. God wants us to be in communion with him on a minute-by-minute, hour-by-hour, and day-by-day basis. When we try and use Him as a last resort, not only are we depriving ourselves of wonderful counsel on a constant basis, but we are also cheapening the relationship. It is little wonder that when we only call out to God when desperate we may often feel that He is not listening. We haven't created the type of personal relationship that fosters a total dependence on Him in every aspect of our lives. When we grow to trust Him in the little things of our lives, we are better equipped and better connected when the inevitability of life's significant crises confronts us.

Fifth, real prayer engenders real love. If we can pray with all sincerity for good fortune for those who have harmed us, we have reached a Christian maturity that will permeate our everyday lives. This love of our enemies is a true sign of spiritual maturity. It is pretty easy for us to think first of ourselves and our needs when we enter into prayer. In that respect we are no different from the five-year-old grandchild who is constantly asking a doting grandparent to buy them every toy in the store. But just as that grandchild will hopefully mature and realize that he or she is not the center of the universe, we as Christians should grow in our faith and realize that our maturation in Christ yields an outward change in our focus from ourselves to those in need around us—including our enemies.

There is much more that can be said about prayer, but as indicated, these are only introductory thoughts on the role of spiritual disciplines in the context of spiritual retreat. Although prayer is certainly the most critical of these disciplines, we will now spend some time looking at other spiritual practices that will benefit us in growth to spiritual maturity and serve as catalysts to recovering our spiritual poise.

Meditation

The role of meditation has gotten a bad rap among many in the Protestant community. Unfortunately, that is because we have heard of the word primarily in the context of Eastern meditative practices as observed in Hinduism, Buddhism, Taoism, and other formal religious movements or in such secular versions as transcendental meditation, made popular in the 1970s and '80s. Common to each of these versions of mediation is a goal to alter or induce a mode of consciousness that is characterized by a feeling of wellness or bliss. Often, those who practice this form of meditation will utilize mantras (repeated phrases or words) or other devices such as prayer beads or a particular stance to allow them to systematically empty their minds of routine thoughts to achieve this "elevated" state of consciousness.

As meditation is contemplated in this book, it is in a distinctly different fashion than described above. Whereas those practicing Eastern meditative practices are seeking to empty their minds, those who practice Christian meditative practices are attempting to fill their minds with the singular subject of God and His Word. These thoughts are contained even in the word *meditation* itself. The English word comes from the Latin word *meditatio* meaning "to think, contemplate, devise or ponder."[117] But just what are we to meditate upon? Again, the Bible presents us with some very clear guidance.

The word *meditate* or *meditation* appears twenty times in the Bible, all but two of those times in the Old Testament. In fact, it appears fifteen times in Psalms, in particular Psalm 119, where it appears seven times. In Psalm 119, we are advised collectively to meditate on Gods "precepts" (15, 78), "statutes" (23, 48) and "words" (148). Reviewing what God has to say, we are admonished to spend our time meditating on the entire word of God as contained in the Holy Bible.

This fundamental principle was recognized by the early monks, and *Lectio Divina*, or divine reading, has been practiced since the sixth century by the Benedictines and other religious orders. In the twelfth century the monk Guigo II formalized this practice of divine reading in to four steps of a "ladder." The four steps of Lectio Divina are as follows.

(1) Read: select a passage and carefully read through it.

(2) Ponder: reflect on the meaning of the particular Scripture you have selected.

(3) Pray: ask God to give you particular insights in to the Scripture selected and incorporate the meaning into your life.

(4) Contemplate: ruminate on the Scripture selected to see how it can be applied in your life and be integrated into Scripture as a whole.[118]

Again, this deep reflection on a small portion of Scripture can lead to new insights and enlightenments that can be particularly helpful in building up your spiritual life. Often this type of meditative reading of Scripture can be achieved when practiced in a retreat setting, where it can be integrated with the other spiritual disciplines discussed in this chapter.

Study

While the difference between study and meditation can appear at first glance to be nuanced, they are in fact very distinct spiritual practices. We study with a particular goal in mind. We are attempting to acquire new knowledge that will enable us to better understand something and hopefully to be able to better explain it as well. When we meditate, we do not have a particular outcome in mind. Rather, we are leaving our minds open to how God will fill it. As explained by Richard Foster in his classic *Celebration of Discipline*,

> The process that occurs in study should be distinguished from meditation. Meditation is devotional; study is analytical. Meditation will relish a word; study will explicate it. Although meditation and study often overlap and function concurrently, they constitute two distinct experiences. Study provides a certain objective framework within which mediation can successfully function.[119]

Perhaps the difference might be made more concrete by examining 2 Timothy 2:15 as translated in the King James Version of the Bible: "Study to show thyself approved unto God, a workman that need not be ashamed, rightly dividing the word of truth." Although a deep and thoughtful reading of the Bible occurs in both meditation and study, the steps that occur after the reading are somewhat different, as are the intended results. Whereas Lectio Divina is expressed in the steps of pondering, praying, and contemplating upon the reading of Scripture, study will involve concentration, comprehension, and reflection.

When we study, we read with a focus and concentration on the subject matter that is much more purposeful then we are merely reading for pleasure. We may read a passage multiple times to ensure that we are gathering each possible nuance of each word as we formulate what the work is trying to tell us. We want to maximize our comprehension of the subject matter we are reviewing so that it enhances our knowledge base and can be recalled at some point in the future. Study becomes a lot like playing with building blocks. As we expand the number of blocks we have available to us, we can then link them together to build ever more complex structures of thought. Ultimately, when reflecting on the cumulative knowledge base we have built, we are able to come up with new and original thought in the area of our study. When this is done in the context of studying our faith, the growth in our spiritual maturity is exponential.

The Bible talks about this hierarchy of learning numerous times. Alternatively the words *knowledge, wisdom,* and *understanding* are utilized. To a casual reader, these may appear to be nearly synonymous. However, a more detailed analysis (or study) will yield subtle and not so subtle differences in meaning. For example, look at Exodus 35:30–31 in the King James Version.

> And Moses said unto the children of Israel. See the lord hath called by name Bezaleel the son of Uri, the son of Hur, of the tribe of Judah; and he hath filled him with the spirit of God, in wisdom, in understanding, and in knowledge, and in all manner of workmanship.

Bezaleel had been appointed by God to be the lead craftsman in the construction of the tabernacle, and God filled him with wisdom, understanding, and knowledge. God was saying more than that Bezaleel was really smart or really gifted. In fact, if you review other translations of these passages, a pattern begins to develop. When you study intently, there is a threefold learning process that takes place. At first you obtain knowledge of the subject. You know the facts that are relevant and make up the body of information on the topic. Next, as you continue to study, you develop an understanding of the topic as a whole. You begin to link the facts together and to be able to differentiate between what is critical and what is secondary. Finally, you gain wisdom on the topic. You not only can express a coherent "wholeness" of the subject, but you can begin to think creatively about the subject and further the understanding of the topic by having original and creative thoughts that add the collective knowledge of the subject.

So it is when Christians study the Word of God and the classic writings of the faith. We begin to be able to do more than quote Bible verses or restate general doctrinal statements. We begin to see how various verses of the Bible relate to each other and how they support in the megastory of creation, fall, and redemption. Eventually, after enough time and study and aided by knowledgeable and trustworthy teachers, we are in a position where we can explain the gospel coherently and demonstrate the ability to handle the Word of God with faithfulness and compassion.

Fasting

Fasting is widely endorsed in the Bible and widely practiced by virtually every major religion of the world. The Bahá'í Faith, Buddhism, Hinduism, Islam, Jainism, Judaism, Sikhism, Taoism, and virtually every denomination of the Christian faith have fast days built in to their liturgical calendar. Yet for all of this history around the practice, it is probably the least understood and practiced (or at least well practiced) spiritual discipline. Before delving in to the biblical admonition to fast and variations of the practice, it is worthwhile to spend some time discussing what the practice of fasting is not.

Fasting is not a method of dieting. Although a reduced caloric intake may lead to a loss of weight, a focus on the ancillary benefits of fasting derived by the participant would be a misdirection of the primary purposes of fasting.

Fasting is not intended as a punishment of the body because of the sinful nature of the flesh. Again, this would be a misdirection of the primary focus of the practice of Christian fasting.

Fasting is not intended to be practiced in isolation from the other spiritual disciplines. Indeed, as will be discussed, fasting is almost universally undertaken in conjunction with one or more of the other spiritual disciplines.

What then is Christian fasting? One author defines it simply as "the voluntary denial of something for a specific period of time, for a spiritual purpose, by an individual, family, community or nation."[120] Certainly the key elements are contained within this definition. The action is voluntary, not compulsory. Denial of food to a prisoner is certainly a reduction in caloric intake but would not be considered the Christian practice of fasting. It is also the denial of something. Although in this short section we will focus on the denial of food and liquids, you could create a fasting from any number of items—sleep, technology, sex, television—that can be distractions preventing spiritual growth. It is also temporary in nature and for a defined period of time. Although one could make fasting a regular part of one's spiritual routine, any given instance should always have a fixed period of duration that has been selected upon the commencement of any particular fast.

The key to the definition is that the fast has as its primary focus the opportunity to experience an increased awareness of God in our lives and to engender spiritual growth. By denying ourselves the topic of much earthly attention (the food we eat) we are opening up to the opportunity to refocus on the spiritual parts of our lives. Fasting, although obviously an exercise involving the individual, can also be a community activity, particularly when the family or community as a whole is seeking guidance or attempting to reestablish a broken relationship with God.

A quick survey of biblical passages on fasting can further clarify and expand the definition and uses of a period of fasting.

- In Deuteronomy 9:7–21 Moses entered two back-to-back forty-day fasts. One was just prior to receiving the Ten Commandments, and the other was after he broke the tablets in anger upon returning to the Israelite camp and finding them worshiping a false god. Fasting prior to a major decision and when seeking guidance is appropriate, as is fasting as a methodology for asking forgiveness for wrongdoing.

- In Psalm 35:13 David advocates fasting as a method for humbling the soul and bringing oneself under the leadership of the Holy Spirit.

- King Jehoshaphat ordered a fast in the country in celebration of a significant victory over their enemies (2 Chronicles 2:3).

- A fast was often called by a prophet in the Old Testament to avert the potential judgment of God when the Israelites had fallen away from worship to the one true God (Joel 1:24, 2:12; Jonah 3:7)

- Paul, upon his conversion on the road to Damascus, did not eat for three days as he sought God's direction in his life (Acts 9:9).

- Paul and Barnabas fasted prior to appointing elders (Acts 14:23).

- And in probably the most well-known passage describing someone fasting, Jesus fasted for forty days and forty nights just as he was about to commence His ministry on earth (Matthew 4:2; Luke 4:2).

Even a cursory review of these verses provides some insights as to when might be an appropriate time to enter into a fast. When seeking guidance from God, prior to undertaking a significant task or opportunity, in realization that you have acted contrary to God's desire and will, and in thanksgiving for deliverance from an evil are all occasions when a fast would be appropriate.

Just like in all of the spiritual disciplines, when one has limited or no experience with fasting, you should follow some common sense guidelines.

(1) Be reasonable in setting the parameters of your fast. Just as you would not attempt a marathon when you have never run a ten-kilometer race, you would not attempt a forty-day total fast on your initial attempt. One-, three-, seven-, and forty-day fasts are all given in the Bible as examples of potential fasting periods (see Judges 20:26, Esther 4:16, 1 Samuel 31:13, and Matthew 4, respectively). Certainly setting your initial fast for a twenty-four-hour period is a reasonable goal.

(2) Consider your schedule when determining your period for a fast. Ideally, you should have limited obligations during the fasting period. You want to be able to pray, meditate on God's Word, and generally be open to God's direction and guidance. Attempting a fast on a busy day filled with work, ball games, elder meetings and other obligations would likely lead to limited benefit in the area of spiritual growth. In addition, you need to recognize that until you become accustomed to the cycle of a fast, your body will initially feel somewhat weakened. You likely may feel a little cranky, so don't compound your problem by attempting to accomplish a significant amount of physical labor. You are robbing yourself of time to focus on the Lord.

(3) Tell only those who you feel need to know that you are on a fast. In Matthew 6:16–18 Jesus warned His followers of the

temptation to fast just to gain the admiration of those around them and advised them to fast in private. Again, this will be easier to do if you haven't scheduled an overly booked day with a lot of contact with third parties.

(4) Do not fill your time of withdrawal from food with a feast of media. Filling your time with videos or television not only steals time better spent with the Lord but will also likely prove to be a temptation to break the fast as you observe the media focused on food consumption.

(5) Be still and at peace with the Lord. Do not set ambitious goals for Bible or other reading. Put aside the normal tendency to schedule a day full of projects. Be open to His leading. Rest in the Lord and listen to what His direction is for you in your life.

As we discussed earlier, fasting usually is not a standalone activity. It is often combined with other spiritual disciplines, such as prayer. The next section of this chapter will review another set of spiritual disciplines that are very complementary to a period of fasting: solitude and silence.

Solitude and Silence

In a society that admires busyness and boldness, the twin spiritual practices of solitude and silence appear to be out of touch with modern times. We are a society that demands we maximize the use of every minute of every day, and *productivity* is the key word of that vocabulary. But under that environment we are prone to fall to the tyranny of the urgent. We feel compelled to address the urgent matters that lie immediately before us instead of the important matters of eternal significance. In such an environment the ideas of being apart from others and being silent and undistracted is so countercultural they appear to be nothing more than antiquated customs from a time before iPods, cable television, and satellite radio. Yet the need to be alone and wait on direction from the Lord has never been greater. This time alone opens us up to a huge opportunity for spiritual growth and reflection.

The disciplines of solitude and silence should be practiced together for maximum benefit. As Richard Foster says,

> We must understand the connection between inner solitude and inner silence. The two are inseparable. All of the masters of the interior life speak of the two in the same breath. For example, The Imitation of Christ which has been the unchallenged masterpiece of devotional literature for five hundred years has a section titled, "On the Love of Solitude and Silence." Dietrich Bonhoeffer makes the two an inseparable whole in Life Together as does Thomas Merton in Thoughts on Solitude.[121]

While we can certainly have periods of silence when in community and periods of solitude without the accompanying silence, by using them in tandem, we open up the door for a closer relationship with God.

Once again, we have numerous examples in Scripture of the purpose and value of time spent alone in quiet reflection. As mentioned above, Jesus Christ began his earthly ministry with forty days of solitude, asking God for direction and preparing for the ministry to come. In Mark 6:31–32, Jesus advised His disciples, "'Come away by yourselves to a desolate place and rest a while,' for many were coming and going, and they had no leisure even to eat. And they went away in the boat to a desolate place by themselves."

Have you ever had days when the demands of work, family, or ministry are so persistent that you did not even have time to grab lunch? In the flesh, our normal reaction in such a situation is to skip lunch and double our efforts to get things done. However, that is just falling into the trap Satan has set for us. We believe that only we can handle the issues of the day, so instead of turning our eyes toward our Creator, we fall right back in to the trap of the tyranny of the urgent.

Do not be confused about the benefits of the practice of solitude and silence. On the surface, these times sound like they could be a time of pure rest and relaxation—a vacation for the soul. Although there certainly will be some of this element of spiritual renewal, they should also be a time of deep reflection and soul searching. "We can only survive solitude," warned Dallas Willard, "if we cling to Christ."[122] Without all of the distractions of other people, media, entertainment, and busyness, we will come face-to-face with our inner selves. Without Christ there to keep us company, it could be a very scary journey. This will be particularly true for those individuals who are natural extroverts. Without the presence of your normal support group, this time alone could turn in to a period of anxiety, reduced energy, and even depression. With all of this in mind, here are a few practical suggestions.

(1) Just like with fasting, the practice of true solitude and silence should be attempted initially in small ways. Perhaps an eight-hour increment would be a reasonable start. A second or third attempt might be for a twenty-four-hour period. Eventually you may want to attempt a week away. The early church fathers practiced years of silence and solitude in the desert, but those examples are not the norm nor, or are they required for us to receive benefits in terms of spiritual growth.

(2) Intermediate periods of practicing these disciplines can best be realized in environments that are conducive to such periods of silence and solitude. Outdoor areas such as the woods, lakes, or oceans can help us avoid the distractions that come from a more urban environment. Retreat centers that have a lot of outdoor spaces are ideal.

(3) Stating the obvious, periods of solitude are best done alone— or at least away from a lot of familiar faces. The temptation to break periods of silence or even to communicate in a nonverbal way is only too human an occurrence when one tries to practice solitude in a group setting.

(4) Simply to refrain from talking is not really achieving spiritual silence. If our minds are racing in every direction and we fail to focus on listening for God's word and direction, we really won't achieve the desired results. The real purpose of silence and solitude is to draw nearer to God. Take these periods of time away and alone to practice some of the other spiritual disciplines, such as prayer, contemplation, and study to bring focus to your period of solitude and silence.

(5) Do not be fanatical. If things need to be said during your period of silence—particularly regarding matters of health or safety—please speak up. The intent is not to make the exercise painful or uncomfortable. With practice, these times away with the only conversation occurring between you and the Lord should be periods to be anticipated. Don't spoil a lifetime of growth and development because of a perceived rigidity that is required in order to be "truly spiritual." Our loving God will meet you where you are.

Summary

The practice of spiritual disciplines should be a part of any maturing Christian's spiritual life. In this chapter we have focused primarily on those disciplines that can be practiced as part of an individual spiritual retreat. Certainly all of the disciplines discussed can be practiced in environments other than a retreat setting. However, when coupled with the appropriate retreat environment, they can assist in jump-starting your spiritual development. Prayer, meditation, study, fasting, solitude, and silence are all complementary to each other as well as to a sacred space where they can be practiced in a more focused and disciplined fashion. Time spent away from your normal routine and with a solitary focus on developing your relationship with the Lord will yield benefits that will last you throughout the rest of your life.

Chapter 7: This All Sounds Good, but Is It Biblical?

At this point, you may be wondering, "This all sounds pretty good, but is it biblical? I mean, after all, it sounds fairly self-centered—almost narcissistic. I keep hearing about my spiritual development, but what does God and His Word have to say about all of this?" I am glad you asked.

The practice of spiritual retreat is evidenced throughout the Bible. From Abraham in the book of Exodus through John and the book of Revelation, biblical characters have drawn away from society in order to receive direction from and grow closer to God. Just a cursory review of two individuals from the Bible—one in the Old Testament and one in the New Testament—can give us tremendous insights in to the biblical appropriateness of spiritual retreat.

Moses

In Exodus 3 we find Moses visiting Mount Sinai for the first time as he is tending his father-in-law's sheep in the wilderness. It was during this period of isolation that God appeared to him as a "flame of fire out of a bush ... that was not consumed."[123] God then first spoke to Moses and gave him His command to return to Egypt to take his people home to the Promised Land. Moses returned to Mount Sinai in Exodus 19 and it is there that Moses received the Ten Commandments and instructions on the construction of the temple.

Contained within these episodes are key elements of true spiritual retreat.

(1) Retreat can lead to the receipt of spiritual gifts. During Moses' two encounters on Mount, Sinai God imparted both wisdom and commands. He gave Moses spiritual direction and responded to questions that Moses posed. Although we don't necessarily have to depart for retreat during periods of searching in our lives, during this time away from our normal routine, God may (and often does) take advantage of our singular focus to clarify His plan for us.

(2) Although retreat may be a time of separation from others, it is a time of concentrated togetherness with God. During Moses time on Sinai, Exodus records some of the most direct interaction that any man has had with God our Creator. God first revealed to Moses His sacred name Yahweh. He physically reached down and gave Moses the carved stone tablets containing the Ten Commandments. He instructed Moses with great precision on how to construct God's home on earth. Few individuals have or will have such a direct physical presence before God, but all of us can reach out and experience God's presence in a more fruitful and meaningful way in our lives.

(3) Retreat is best achieved in special surroundings accompanied by special behavior. Moses was required to follow God's command to take off his sandals as he approached Him at the burning bush. The mountain contained a rugged beauty that symbolically elevated him closer to heaven. Retreat for us can best be achieved when we leave all of our earthly trappings behind us and join God in a space that is indicative of both God's beauty and His majesty.

Moses was only one in a long line of Old Testament prophets who took time away to have a greater connectivity to God. The lives of Abraham, Isaac, and Joseph all had episodes where they were set apart for a time of special interaction with God. So did Peter, Paul, and John in the New Testament. But perhaps the clearest example of an individual who took time away from the world around him in order to have a period of focused time of reflection and prayer is the example of Jesus Christ himself.

Jesus Christ

As in all things in life, Jesus can serve as the example to Christians of how to lead a life that has the element of spiritual retreat deeply imbedded in it. Just some of the verses outlining his call for retreat are listed below.

- "And rising very early in the morning, while it was still dark, he departed and went out to a desolate place, and there he prayed" (Mark 1:35).

- "And he said to them, 'Come away by yourselves to a desolate place and rest a while'" (Mark 6:31).

- "But when you pray, go into your room and shut the door and pray to your Father who is in secret. And your Father who sees in secret will reward you" (Mathew 6:5—Jesus' Sermon on the Mount).

- "And after he dismissed the crowds, he went up on the mountain by himself to pray" (Mathew 14:23).

- Probably the most well known of the passages discussing Jesus during a period of retreat occurs in Luke 4:1–2: "And Jesus, full of the Holy Spirit, returned from the Jordan and was led by the Spirit in to the wilderness for forty days, being tempted by the devil. And he ate nothing during those days, and when it ended he was hungry."

We know that at the conclusion of this long period of retreat and fasting, Satan attempted to short-circuit God's plan for redemption by tempting Jesus three times. However, at the conclusion of these temptations, it is written in Matthew 4:11, "Then the devil left him, and behold, angels came and were ministering to him." At this point, the official ministry of Jesus Christ commences.

From this story of the temptation of Christ we can draw valuable lessons regarding the need for retreat in our lives.

(1) A spiritual retreat is the ideal time to seek God's guidance for your life. This is particularly true when you are seeking or sense a change in life direction. This time alone in contemplative prayer can prove extremely illuminating. When you separate yourself from your normal routine and related distractions, you are the most open and vulnerable to the leadings of the Holy Spirit. Pray that God will give you wisdom and then listen with a sincere heart to the telltale answer.

(2) During this time alone, you are also potentially vulnerable to the misleading of Satan. As long as you are preoccupied by the everyday distractions of this world, Satan has little to fear. When you make a sincere effort to isolate yourself and focus on listening for God to speak in your life, Satan has a reason to be concerned. Satan loves complacent and self-righteous individuals who take no time for self-reflection and personal growth. When you are vulnerable to the leadings of the Holy Spirit, if you are not careful, you could also be vulnerable to Satan's deceptive lies. This is particularly true if you conduct your time of retreat in a haphazard fashion. In the next chapter we will discuss some common forms of adding structure to your time alone. Just sitting in a corner and letting your mind wander and wishing for guidance will be unproductive at best and potentially damaging at worse.

(3) The practice of the spiritual disciplines is an excellent way to ensure that you derive the most benefit from your time away. Again, Jesus Christ sets the example. He prayed and fasted during His forty days in the wilderness. Very few of us will ever undertake a forty-day retreat, much less a forty-day fast. However, within the limits of our own physical capabilities, a time of fasting accompanied with a time of prayer should yield positive results.

(4) Retreat is a time for us to be spiritually renewed and equipped to lead a more productive spiritual life. Retreat is a time to regain our spiritual poise and come away refreshed and with a clearer vision of God's plan for our lives. It is also a time to come away with a renewed focus and energized to do God's work. Immediately after Jesus concluded His retreat, He began his ministry. As will be discussed in the next chapter, we should come away from a period of retreat with a call to action and renewed focus on living the dynamic Christian life. None of us are called to save the world, but we are certainly expected to impact that small piece of it that God has given us dominion over.

Objections to the Path of Spiritual Retreat

As discussed in the beginning chapters of this book, many people in the Protestant community have given little thought to the concept of spiritual retreat. They may view it as an anachronistic practice having little applicability to the "modern" Christian's life. Up to this point, most of the book has been focused on dispelling this attitude. However, there is a segment of the Christian world that has examined "spirituality" and "retreat" and come to the conclusion that such efforts are not only out of step but also are potentially a distraction from obtaining true spiritual maturity. In general, the objections fall in to three categories.

(1) An over emphasis on spirituality is in actuality another form of Gnosticism. A radical expression of personal spirualty is a form of the ancient heresy of Gnosticism—the belief that only those that know the "secret sacred ways" are truly saved.

(2) An inward focus on one's personal spiritual growth detracts from the true work of the gospel—reaching out to those who are suffering and in need of the God's redemptive grace. To quote the old adage, "They are so heavenly minded they are of no earthly good."

(3) We are saved only through the belief in Jesus Christ as our Lord and Savior. This emphasis on spiritual disciplines and time away in isolation leads to a type of salvation that has at its core a works-based message of redemption.

Each of these objections will be examined in some detail below, but suffice it to say that there is some confusion about what some writers have defined as classical spirituality versus biblical spirituality versus New Age spirituality. So in addressing these questions, it will be helpful to have a working definition of all three of these terms.[124]

Classical spirituality has as its focus developing a Christian mysticism in an adherent. As a mystic, the adherent has as a goal the perfection of the soul, the suppression of earthly desires, and an all-encompassing union with God. This growth is inclined to be highly introspective, for the true path to the discovery of God resides in the interior of the self. Classical mysticism espouses a philosophy of self-denial and asceticism as the path to biblical faith. Often the adherents will practice their spiritual disciplines in long-term isolation like the early hermits and monks of the church. There is an almost hyperreligiosity to the virtual exclusion of any other activities in life. Among those individuals who would exemplify this tradition would be Bernard of Clairvaux, Catherine of Siena, or in the more recent past Thomas Merton.

New Age spirituality actually has as its focus not God (or at least the God that we as Christians would recognize) or union with God, but rather purely a discovery of one's own identity. New Age mystics do not seek to adhere themselves to the unchanging Creator of the world, but rather to join the stream of "universal consciousness" that theoretically pulsates through all of creation. Although most often thought of as a product of Eastern meditative religions, New Age spirituality actually has its origins in the Renaissance, Enlightenment, and Romantic periods of Western history. These periods introduced the thought that man is in fact not fallen, but rather capable of almost unlimited potential if he can just learn how to harness the "power within." An external god is not necessary because, in the end, we are all gods ourselves to the extent we can access the life source that is resident within us. Adherents of such a philosophy of life would include G. W. F. Hegel, Martin Heidegger, Ralph Waldo Emerson, and Walt Whitman.

Biblical Spirituality is a spirituality that recognizes that the source of our knowledge of God comes from an encounter between the divine personhood of God and the human person of His creation. God reveals Himself to us through His creation, both the world around us (general revelation) and His Son and His Word (special revelation). "God is not subordinated to the general category of person, but personhood is illumined by God's self-revelation in Jesus Christ."[125] This illumination is made evident in the writings of the Holy Scripture, which tells the story of God's plan for His creation, the fall that separated His creation from Him, and the reconciliation that can only occur through Jesus of Nazareth.

> Evangelical spirituality appeals to a norm outside conscience and experience: God's self-revelation in Jesus Christ. This norm is attested in Scripture and witnessed to in church tradition. The final criterion in this kind of spirituality is the paradoxical unity of Word and Spirit. A place is made for silence, but not as an attempt to get beyond the Word to an effable reality—the undifferentiated unity. Instead, the function of silence in a Biblical context is to prepare us to hear the Word.[126]

Adherents to this type of spirituality include Blaise Pascal, Dietrich Bonhoeffer, J. I. Packer, and T. F. Torrance, among others.

A quick review of these definitions will highlight that New Age spirituality has no real association with a true follower of Christ. While classical spirituality has much to be admired about it with its singular focus on knowing God, it also introduces practices that when carried to an extreme have no basis in the Bible. That being said, as was reviewed in the earlier chapters of this book, there is much that Protestant Christians can and should learn by reviewing the lives of adherents of this more rigorous spirituality.

Certainly biblical spirituality can be recognized as both the most desirable and the most scripturally based behavior. However, although the defined behavior is the most desirable, the integration of practices and disciplines first evidenced in classical spirituality can provide the structure that many (if not all) Christians need in order to achieve this truly biblical spirituality. Having the Word of God as our bellwether against which to test our behavior will enable us to lead passionate, focused, and appropriate spiritual lives.

With this background, let us review the objections listed above.

Is Spirituality a Form of Gnosticism?

Gnosticism has been a plague that has haunted the church from the very beginning of the Christian faith. In fact, conceptually, Gnosticism in some form predates the arrival of Christ. The name *Gnosticism* derives from the Greek word *gnosis,* which means *knowledge.* According to the Gnostics, they possess a special, mystical knowledge that is reserved only for those with "true understanding." That secret knowledge is the key to salvation.

Gnostics believe that the material world is evil (or in some instances not even real). The essence of the human being is an eternal spirit that is imprisoned in an evil physical body. The world is not our true home, but rather an obstacle that must be overcome to reach our true spiritual world. In Gnostic belief, God the Father did not create the world. In fact, depending on the strain of Gnostic faith, there are multiple gods of greater or lesser importance. One of these lesser gods, far removed from the ultimate god, created this fallen material world.

In order for us to escape this physical world, we must receive divine revelation from some spiritual being that can "awaken" our sleeping spirit and prepare us to escape to the spiritual world. These messengers will bring us the gnosis, or knowledge, for this transformative event to occur. In the Christian form of Gnosticism, the spiritual messenger is Jesus Christ.

Since the body and matter are evil, most Christian Gnostics reject the idea that Christ had an earthly body like ours. Depending on the strain of Gnosticism, Christ was either a ghost with the appearance of a human or he was two separate individuals—a heavenly, spiritual Jesus and the physical Christ. For this attitude and other reasons, Gnosticism represents a real challenge to true Christianity.

Those who criticize the "overemphasis" or our spiritual nature argue that this is the first step toward this ancient heresy. There is an aura of elitism that can surround someone who believes that they possess unique access to God through spiritual practices that have been passed on to them from predecessors, or at least that is the potential abuse that is pointed out. After all, didn't Jesus Christ himself condemn the Pharisees for their holier-than-thou attitude?

While all of these arguments have superficial applicability, someone who would actually fall in to one of the above descriptions is not an indictment of the practice of spirituality, but rather an indictment of the individual themselves. Surely if someone does exhibit an attitude of superiority toward other Christians because of his or her focus on spiritual practices, this attitude cannot be condoned. However, someone demonstrating such an attitude has obviously not adhered to the fundamental principles of a truly Spirit-led life. Somewhere in the whole process, such people have reversed the focus of the spiritual practices. They have turned the time alone with God and the solitary focus on our Creator in to a time of focus on themselves. Somewhere along the way, the admonition of Matthew 23:12 and the warning of Matthew 23:13 have been lost.

> Whoever exalts himself will be humbled, and whoever humbles himself will be exalted. But woe to you, scribes and Pharisees, hypocrites! For you neither enter yourselves nor allow those who would enter go in.

True spirituality has in its very essence the solitary focus on our triune God. There is no thought that by entering into a closer communion with God that somehow we are separating ourselves from other followers of Christ. We are still very much sinners, and if anything, spending more time reading Scripture and praying to our heavenly Father will only make us more aware of our condition and more thankful every day for the sacrifice of Jesus on the cross.

The closeness to God that we will hopefully feel as we progress in our spiritual growth is not the result of any special knowledge or insight. Rather, it is knowledge available to any follower of our Messiah who seeks to follow Him. We are just making time in our lives so that we can hear the call and follow it.

Does an Inward Focus Distract Us from Fulfilling God's Great Commission?

The second objection follows this train of thought. But wasn't Christ last command to go forth to all the world and make disciples? If we become inwardly focused, won't we risk separating ourselves from those around us who are in desperate need of the gospel? How can we be so focused on ourselves and our spiritual growth when family and friends are potentially headed to eternal damnation?

The response to this concern rests in truly understanding what we are called to do when we respond to the desire to grow our own spiritual lives and what we are called to do to rescue others. The essence of this dual responsibility is contained in Matthew 22:34–40 when Jesus is asked, "What is the great commandment?" Jesus responds, "You shall love the Lord your God with your whole heart and with your whole soul and with your whole mind. This is the great and first commandment. And a second is like it: You shall love your neighbor as yourself. On these two commandments depends all the Law and the Prophets."

Loving God and wanting to more closely experience His presence in our lives is not incompatible with maintaining an outward-focused concern for those in the world who are less fortunate than us both spiritually and physically. Simply put, it is not an either-or, but rather both. Not only are we to love the Lord God with all that we are—spiritually, physically, and mentally—but we are also to love our fellow man with near equal fervor (near equal, not equal, only because the relationship between creature and creator cannot be duplicated). However, our love for those who are cocreated should be deep and special precisely because they are made in the image of God and by loving and serving those in need, we are in fact loving and serving God. As it states in Matthew 25:40, "As you did it to one of the least of these my brothers, you did it to me." As our walk with God becomes closer, the natural result should not be separation from those around us, but rather a heightened awareness of those around us who are "lost and least." Our passions for our fellow man should be aroused, not hardened.

Part of the reason this concern may exist is that a life overly focused on spiritual matters may have a bad reputation when it comes to community life because of the hermit model outlined by the early desert fathers and certain groups of the early monastic movement. The reality is that the totally isolated hermit was a rare exception. Often, these men and women attracted followers, and community did develop, as was discussed in earlier chapters. Even if these models do appear somewhat devoid of focused outreach to the community at large, as the monastic model developed, they became groups focused on outreach to the poor and forgotten (for example, the Franciscans and Dominicans).

This heritage of monastic communal life coupled with intense community involvement is well demonstrated by the New Monastic Movement. Although a precise origin of this movement is difficult to pinpoint, the phrase "New Monasticism" was coined by Jonathan Wilson in his 1998 book *Living Faithfully in a Fragmented World*.[127] Wilson in turn was building on thoughts of philosopher Alasdair MacIntryre and theologian Deitrich Bonhoeffer.

Wilson proposed four principles that would underpin this new form of monasticism: (1) it would be "marked by a recovery of the telos (purpose) of this world ... to bring the whole of life under the lordship of Christ"; (2) it would be aimed at all of God's people and not draw a distinction between those operating in a secular versus sacred professions; (3) there would be a discipline applied, not in the sense of the old monastic rules, but rather by the voluntary and joyful amalgamation of a small group living in mutual accountability to each other; and (4) it would be "undergirded by deep theological reflection and commitment," which would allow the church to recover its primary role as a witness to the world.[128]

Communities based upon these ideals have been formulated in inner-city communities in Philadelphia, Pennsylvania; Harrisonburg, Virginia; Durham, North Carolina; and several other communities. These members do not wear special garb nor take the traditional monastic vows of celibacy, poverty, and obedience. They do share certain common "marks," as defined in the Rutba House community manifesto.[129]

(1) Relocation to "abandoned places at the margin of society"

(2) Sharing economic resources with fellow community members

(3) Hospitality to strangers

(4) Active pursuit of just reconciliation between the races

(5) Humble submission to Christ's body, the church

(6) Intentional formation in the way of Christ and the rule of the community along the line of the old novitiate

(7) Nurturing common life among members of this intentional community

(8) Support for celibate singles along with monogamous married couples and their children

(9) Geographic proximity to community members who share a common rule of life

(10) Care for the land given to the community along with support of local economies

(11) Peacemaking in the midst of violence and conflict resolution within communities

(12) Commitment to a disciplined, contemplative life

While I am not advocating that every Christian should be an active participant in the New Monastic movement, it is refreshing to note that there is certainly nothing incompatible between leading a disciplined, contemplative life and still leading a life of Christian service. To the contrary, leading a life of careful reflection, study, and prayer would only sensitize you to the biblical mandate to care for the poor and hurting in this world. To believe otherwise would be to have a warped view of the purpose of a follower of Christ.

Does an Emphasis on Spirituality Create a Works-Based Plan of Salvation?

We are told in Paul's letter to the Ephesians, "For by grace you have been saved through faith. And this is not of your own doing; it is the gift of God, not a result of works so that no one may boast" (Ephesians 2:8–9). At the same time, James told us, "What good is it, my brother, if someone says he has faith but does not have works? Can that faith save him?" (James 2:14). At first these two verses can appear to be contradictory, but the answer lies in the definition of *faith* in each verse.

When people says they have faith or belief in something they can really be saying one of two things. First, they can be saying that they believe that something is true. This is a statement of fact. The existence of a proposition is held to be correct. However, that type of faith is not the type that can lead to salvation. As James says, "You believe that God is one; you do well. Even the demons believe and shudder" (James 2:19). A person who smokes cigarettes can hardly deny that smoking will be harmful to one's health. It is an indisputable fact. However, that does not lead to everyone stopping smoking. On the contrary, millions of people still smoke, as feeding the short-term addiction to smoking is more compelling to them than acting on their knowledge of smoking as a detriment to their health and immediately stopping. In the same light, millions of people have heard the gospel message clearly articulated to them and yet will fail to act on it by having a clear and meaningful act of conversion.

The second way this concept of having faith can be interpreted is fully trusting and relying on. This goes beyond mere head knowledge but rather leads to a change in attitude and action taken by the hearer. The commitment to the object of the faith is one that involves the entire person—physically, mentally, emotionally, and spiritually. We are not merely acknowledging that a statement is true; we are acting on that knowledge. This is the essence of true Christian conversion. We are indwelled by the Holy Spirit, who strengthens us to act upon our beliefs. This is the type of faith that James was advocating—one that leads to outward signs that we truly believe in the message of salvation. We are not compelled to action because we believe it will lead to our reconciliation and salvation. We are compelled to action because as redeemed people of God we are so thankful for this great gift that we want to show our love and appreciation by imitating as best we can the example set by our Savior Jesus Christ.

With this background, the answer to this third objection to leading the spiritual life becomes obvious. Seeking to lead a more spiritually focused life is not an addition to our confession of faith; it is the outcome of our confession of faith. We do not spend more time in prayer, meditation, reflection, fasting, and the other spiritual disciplines because we believe doing so will secure our faith. We undertake these actions because we desire, as true Christians, to draw nearer to God. We seek to worship the only one who is truly worthy of worship—not because He will love us any more than He already does, but to demonstrate our love to Him.

Likewise, we do not engage in the world and seek to transform it because this will somehow secure our salvation. We seek to transform it because we recognize that it is broken and fallen and not in the state God first created it. We also recognize that the world will not be returned to its designed glory until Christ comes again. But until that day, we do recognize that we are stewards of the gift of this world, and compelled by our love of the Creator, we seek to lessen the damage in any way that we can. Our actions are driven by gratitude. Just as a loving child thanks his parents for a gift by volunteering to help around the house, so we too "volunteer" to lead lives of committed Christians. This is not to ensure our faith, but to demonstrate it.

The evidence seems compelling that leading a more focused spiritual life is not only biblically permissible, but also actually a biblical mandate. Much of the confusion that abounds in the Protestant world regarding spirituality rests in the confusion between some aspects of classical spirituality and what we have termed biblical spirituality. We do not enter into periods of retreat for our own personal growth (although that is hopefully a byproduct) but rather for two very Biblical reasons. First, we enter into spiritual retreat so that we can more thoroughly know and demonstrate our love for the God who created us and provided us with a plan of salvation. Second, we enter into retreat so that through this period of renewal, we can become more effective in fulfilling the biblical mandate to care for God's world, including His greatest act of creation—our fellow men and women who occupy it.

We have spent several chapters discussing the need for retreat, the history of spiritual retreat, the disciplines that can be practiced in retreat, and the biblical mandate for retreat. In the next chapter we will take a step back and with this background answer the questions of how to begin and what to do to experience this life of spiritual retreat.

Chapter 8: So What Do I Do Next?

Hopefully after reading this much of the book, you are beginning to believe that this spiritual retreat thing might actually be worth trying. So what is your next step? From practical experience, the most difficult but absolutely most imperative thing needs to occur—you need to make time in your schedule to participate in a retreat. One of the most frustrating things encountered by those that run retreat centers is the number of people with great motives and purpose who, despite the purest of intentions, never schedule a retreat or schedule one and then cancel.

Just as in many other areas of life, the urgent matters of the day appear to dominate the most precious resource anyone has: time. Doing it tomorrow becomes doing it next week, then next month, and then next year. Almost without a struggle we forfeit the opportunity to regain our spiritual poise and reorient our lives around our God and Savior. Once again the tyranny of the urgent has emerged victorious. Resolve, as soon as you finish reading this chapter, to identify when and where you will take this sabbatical for the soul. Then make the arrangements. Now that you are all fired up, the next couple of questions that will come to mind are (1) "How much time am I talking about?" and (2) where should I go for this retreat? The third, obvious question ("What should I do when I am on retreat?") will be the topic of the next chapter.

What Are My Options on Time?

When someone is asked to commit to something, one of the first question expressed before responding is "How long will this take?" It would be easy to give a trite response like "as long as it takes!" While that may be true in the abstract sense, to be of the most use I will seek to give some practical guidance in this area.

Individual retreats can last for as short as a day to up to thirty days (or theoretically longer). Although certainly you want to allow for enough time to effectively decompress from your day-to-day activity and have ample time to spend in prayer and the other spiritual disciplines, you should also be realistic about the time commitment you can make. We are all in different stages of life. Certainly the young married couple with small children will not have as much flexibility in their schedule as a single, retired person. The same is true for our spiritual lives. Although retreat can benefit anyone regardless of his or her stage of spiritual development, the individual who has been in retreat numerous times before is in a better position to undertake a lengthy period of retreat than a newcomer to the Christian faith.

This book has been written with the novice retreater in mind. While those who have experienced the benefits of spiritual retreat before hopefully learned from some of the earlier chapters covering the historical and biblical precedents for retreat, questions of length and location may be of less practical importance. With that in mind, here are a few suggestions on what to consider when establishing a time frame for your retreat.

(1) Honestly assess your ability to be away from your day-to-day obligations. The key word is *honestly*. Many of us operate under the exaggerated assumption that people at work or at home cannot survive without us. While this attitude may be temporarily ego gratifying, the reality is that those around us in life are more capable of dealing with their daily existence than we might have imagined. Remember that this time away

is not only for our benefit, but will also allow us to refocus and reground ourselves in our faith, thus making us more effective in living out our daily lives. Those around us should benefit from our time away by gaining an individual with renewed focus and a more Christlike heart.

(2) Honestly assess your temperament and account for that in the timing and structure of your retreat. God has created us all with a personality and a proclivity for action or inaction. If you are like the apostle Peter, you are action and activity oriented. You love to have people around you and love to engage in conversation and debate. To tackle a thirty-day silent getaway as your first entrée in to the world of spiritual retreat is likely to create a recipe for high anxiety, if not disaster. That is not to say that the only people who can go on retreats are introverted, contemplative types. Rather, if your personality leans to the other extreme, this will be an exercise designed to stretch your comfort zone, and like any exercise activity, you should be relatively conservative as you start out and work to build your endurance.

(3) Honestly assess your spiritual maturity before embarking on a retreat. Someone who has been deeply committed to their faith for decades and has developed an abiding walk with God is merely utilizing the retreat setting to experience an in-depth and concentrated period of personal time with the Lord. Someone who has just come to know the Lord and is just beginning their spiritual walk is likely not prepared to maximize the benefit of an extended spiritual retreat. There is a risk in misunderstanding the point that is being made. Clearly everyone can and will benefit from participating in a retreat. It could be argued that someone brand-new in the faith might benefit even more from a prolonged retreat, as there is so much that the Lord might have to say to them. But a more practical reality is that there is maturing process that occurs when we experience a daily walk

with the Lord. It is comprised of numerous elements, including a committed church life, mentoring from others in the body, and time in study and prayer. An attempt to short-cut the process by plunging oneself in to a prolonged spiritual retreat is likely to be counterproductive. The law of diminishing return will begin to apply. In addition, there is a distinct possibility that by isolating yourself in prolonged spiritual retreat early in your walk, you risk forming some "bad habits" from either your own ignorance or from ideas planted by Satan. To utilize an inexact sports analogy, you aren't likely to benefit as a brand-new beginner in golf from playing golf thirty days in a row. Bad habits that you may have will only become ingrained and need to be unlearned. In addition, sheer fatigue will result in sore muscles, calloused hands, and a lot of frustration that will make you wonder why you ever took up the game! Set a reasonable time frame based on where you are in your spiritual walk.

(4) Discuss your intentions of making a spiritual retreat with those around you who will be impacted by your absence. Although there can obviously be exceptions for emergencies, as will be discussed in the next chapter, time away for retreat should be singularly focused on building your relationship with your heavenly Father. Repeated interruptions during this absence will prove the type of distraction that could undermine a lot of the potential value of the retreat itself. Although you may have a clear understanding of the need for the time away and the value of the investment being made, others around you will likely be less certain. Particularly in the case of spouses, seek their input on the appropriate time away.

(5) We have mentioned twice already the risk of setting too ambitious a goal for your time away. There should also be equal caution against limiting your time so narrowly that very little true time for growth occurs. Certainly nonresidential day retreats can have immense value. But a steady diet of these miniretreats

without allowing for a longer period away will prove a potential limiting factor in your spiritual growth. With rare exceptions, most people cannot leave the day-to-day distractions and issues of life behind them instantaneously upon departing for a retreat. There is almost always a period of decompression that must occur. You need ample time to practice the spiritual disciplines in a conscientious and sincere way. You need ample time for God to communicate with you. This is not a process that you can dictate the timing of any more so than you could dictate the timing of any other personal relationship you are seeking to create. Just as a series of short naps are not a substitute for a good solid night of sleep, neither is a two- or three-hour "prayer time" a substitute for a residential retreat.

With these factors as background, there are a few historic patterns that have developed regarding time frames for a spiritual retreat.

The Three-Day Retreat

Balancing the demands of daily life with the command to love and know your God, a popular form of retreat has become the three-day retreat. Part of the reason this has become accepted is the pragmatic reality that with the addition of one personal day in combination with a weekend, many working individuals can more easily fit this time frame into their schedule. In addition, three days facilitates a period of decompression, a period of contemplation, and a period of reflection.

This format is particularly prevalent in the Roman Catholic tradition. Originating in Spain in 1944, this three-day movement (or *Cursillo*) has become an integral part of the lay religious movement with Catholics. The traditional format consists of fifteen talks that you can take back with you and apply what you have learned (at the end, on the "fourth day"). These sessions take various forms depending on the age and life circumstances of the participants. Variations of the Cursillo have also been adopted by the Anglican and Presbyterian denominations as well.

Without commenting on the content of these sessions, the time frame does offer an example that attempts to balance the competing demands of family, profession, and faith. There is also another reason why the concept of a three-day retreat over a weekend represents a model that not only is convenient, but also has as its roots the cycle of Christ's redemptive act.

> In Christian symbolism, Friday is the day of death, of letting go. On Friday we surrender to God's call of love and to our own wish for transformation through Christ. Saturday begins the process of renewal, a time of reflection, repentance, and metanoia. Sunday is the day of resurrection, on which we rejoice in our newfound life. This tri-fold template, sanctified by Christ's holy example, has inspired millions of men and women throughout the centuries. I believe that we make a wise choice by adopting it for our retreat.[130]

Certainly for the retreat beginner, the three-day weekend retreat offers a reasonable compromise between the competing demands of real life and the benefits of a prolonged opportunity to reach deep and commune richly with our Lord. The structure of a three-day retreat as part of a Christian's annual cycle of life would seem to be at least a reasonable starting point to incorporate into one's spiritual growth. For those desiring to drink even deeper from the wellspring of these ancient practices, certainly additional days can be added on to the stay. Before addressing the next introductory question, it would be worth a brief look at another time-related example of a retreat format.

The Spiritual Exercises of Saint Ignatius

When we discuss the matter of content of a spiritual retreat, we will return in detail to the activities contained within the spiritual exercises of Saint Ignatius. Suffice to say at this point in time that Saint Ignatius is well known as the founder of the Society of Jesus (Jesuits). He lived in the sixteenth century during the Counter-Reformation. Born into an aristocratic family, he was severely injured during the Battle of Pamplona in 1521 and underwent a spiritual revival during his recovery after reading *The Imitation of Christ*. He renounced his military career and, inspired by Francis of Assisi, began a life of contemplative prayer and study. Between 1524 and 1537 he studied theology in Spain and France and in 1541, along with a handful of followers, established the Society of Jesus. During much of the last thirty years of his life, he wrote and then continued to develop a series of spiritual exercises designed to bring the adherent to a deeper relationship with God.[131]

These exercises are divided into four "weeks" of meditations and are often referred to as the thirty-day retreat. The term *week* is flexible in that they may consist of more or less than seven days. This retreat structure has become the norm for many men (and even women) who are involved in the religious orders of the Roman Catholic faith.

As a general outline, the "weeks" relate to the following.[132]

(1) The first week corresponds roughly to what is called the purgative way of spiritual life. The primary focus is on bringing one's spiritual life into order and purifying the soul to prepare one for the remainder of the retreat.

(2) The aim of the second week is to focus on committing to an interior knowledge and love of the person of Jesus Christ so that one is better equipped to identify with Christ and to adapt one's life to the model of Christ.

(3) The third week of the exercises is concerned with the passion of our Lord and confirms in the exercitant that he has chosen to follow Christ more closely by increasing his awareness of Christ's suffering on the cross and our sorrow for his sins.

(4) The fourth week's exercises are designed to focus on the risen life of Christ and to engender one to the unselfish love and joy of Christ's risen glory.

Around this global structure, Ignatius designed a series of prayers, acts, and meditations to focus on our sinfulness and Christ's redemptive act of salvation. Again, in the next chapter we will review some of the content in more detail. At this point it is helpful to note that this framework has been used for centuries on an expandable scale from as little as eight to as many as forty days, providing additional insight into what potential time frames to consider to the question "How much time are we talking about?" As indicated initially, the real answer is "As much time as it takes," but at least we now have some idea of how others before us have answered that question.

What Are My Options on Place?

Where some fairly specific answers have been given to answer the question of "How much?" the answer to the question of "Where?" can only be given in more general terms of describing characteristics versus actual locations. When the search words "retreat center" were recently plugged into an Internet search engine, 12,800,000 results popped up. Specifying "religious retreat centers" narrows the search to a more manageable 4,190,000 hits. Enter "Christian retreat centers," and the number drops in half to about two million hits. There are specialty websites such as *Retreat Finder* and *Find the Divine* that can assist you in narrowing your search even further. Or you can narrow your search geographically, as almost every state in the Union has a website for retreat centers within its borders. So at first glance, it would appear that there is a booming business in the area of providing accommodations for individuals looking for a place to have their souls nourished.

The reality is that given the number of professing Christians in the United States, there are not really as many qualified retreat centers as one would think. Part of the confusion exists because of muted meaning of *retreat* among most Christians. When the context is the typical men's or women's church retreat offered by most churches, then any hotel or camp that can accommodate a large group of people and provide for a centralized lecture hall will fit the bill. When looking for a location that will provide the opportunity for the type of deep, reflective, individualized retreat that this book is advocating, the choices are likely to be much more limited. However, even in the less populated areas of the country, there are likely to be at least a handful within reasonable driving distance for an extended weekend retreat.

Utilizing the author's home state of Indiana as an example, there are twenty-eight locations that advertise themselves as Christian retreat centers. Nearly half of these are camps or other large facilities more structured around large group outings. Of the remaining fifteen that appear more suited for individual retreat, ten are run by some order of the Roman Catholic Church, three by other denominations, and two are nondenominational. An unscientific review of several other states reveals that this representation of denominations is not atypical. Approximately two-thirds of retreat centers are owned and operated by a religious order of the Catholic faith. Analyzing this on an "available bedrooms" basis, that percentage rises substantially. Many of these Catholic retreat centers are well established with a long history and often offer dozens of rooming options at each location, compared to most other retreat centers that often only have available a handful of rooms. As we reviewed, the Roman Catholic Church has a long history of personal retreat among its adherents, so having a large presence in the area of facilities would be a natural result.

For those who are not Catholic, this should not be a point of concern. Virtually all of the Catholic retreat centers are very accommodating to those of other faith traditions. The reality is there are a number of other factors other than just the denominational background of the sponsoring group that needs to be considered when evaluating your alternatives and selecting the location for your initial retreat. Among those areas that should be evaluated are:

(1) The nature of the accommodations. Retreat centers can vary considerably in regards to the style of the accommodations. Many are very simple with small rooms, limited furniture, and

virtually no amenities (including private baths). Others provide a more upscale environment with private bathrooms, extensive libraries, exercise facilities, and other near-resort-like amenities. Many will offer an option to have meals included with your room, although many will also provide a room only. You need to again honestly assess what environment will best suit your needs. For some, the simple, dormitory-like rooms offer no concerns and in fact may be welcome, as they can provide limited distractions and greater ease at focusing on the task at hand. Others would prefer a greater degree of privacy and would prefer their own restroom and cooking facilities. There really is no right or wrong answer. Naturally, cost may weigh into your decision as well. The sparser the surroundings, the more likely the costs will be minimized. As a general rule, the costs of the accommodations are usually considerably less than a hotel room in the same geographic vicinity. This is a result of the attitude of the people running the retreat house, who view their effort as a ministry and not a business. In fact, many retreat centers are run by churches or other nonprofit entities.

(2) The size and nature of the facility. Many Catholic retreat centers are operated on the grounds of a larger Catholic institution. There may be a monastery of convent on the grounds. Some are located at colleges or universities. While this can have significant benefits, such as access to libraries or chapels, it also means that you will be more likely to have interaction with both others on retreat as well as others using the grounds for unrelated purposes. If you are seeking a place apart for independent prayer or reflection, you may just have to work a little harder to find it.

Other retreat centers can be quite small, perhaps just a few rooms. There can be a kind of intimacy in the surroundings that can be comforting (or stifling), depending on your personality. What some small retreat centers may lack in size they can make up for in their ability to provide variety in the accommodations.

Just as a home can have more variety than a standardized hotel, a small retreat center can offer variety to suit different needs. Depending on the location of the retreat center, you may also find it easier to get the necessary "alone time" required to make the retreat most beneficial.

(3) The geographic setting of the facility. Although there are several very fine urban retreat centers, many individual retreaters prefer a location that is conducive to the type of contemplative thinking that a spiritual retreat is seeking to engender. As will be discussed in the next chapter, retreats can often be enhanced when accompanied with some type of physical activity, such as a long walk or work in a garden. Obviously, a more rural setting is more accommodating to such activities. Retreat centers located in the woods, in the hills or mountains, or on a body of water can be conducive to stimulating the appropriate mind-set for a successful retreat. Henry David Thoreau did not pick Walden Pond and its surrounding woods to write his contemplative works because of the nightlife.

(4) Accessibility to spiritual directors. The topic of spiritual guides or directors will be covered in detail in the next chapter. At this point consider this an individual who is a cross between a coach and a counselor and can assist in maximizing the experience of your retreat. While many retreat centers will have such individuals on staff, the availability, cost, and functions can vary. If you are desirous of having such an individual at your disposal, this introduces an additional dynamic that needs to be accounted for. In some instances, access to a qualified director can take precedence over other considerations like location and type of facility.

(5) Flexibility in programming. Many retreat centers will organize particular time periods on their schedule to focus on particular programmatic aspects of retreat. Silent versus open retreat is one simple example. In some situations, the sponsor of a structured

retreat will want all the retreatants to attend preretreat sessions to become acquainted with each other and with the curriculum that will be followed. If you are one of those individuals who prefer to keep their schedules flexible (or open to how the Spirit leads them) you may want to defer to a less structured environment.

(6) Attending solo or with companions. Depending on the nature and structure of the retreat, you may want to be accompanied by a friend or spouse. It would not be uncommon for an individual who is new to the practice of retreat to attend his initial retreat with someone who has had prior experience. If nothing else, this can put the novice more at ease since the fear of the unknown can be mitigated through the encouragement of the companion. Retreat is still very much an individual endeavor, but finding time to reflect upon the retreat activities together can be a strong reinforcement of the principles learned. When selecting the retreat facility, account for this desire to meet and talk with your companion. If this companion also happens to be your spouse, just ensure that the center has accommodations for married participants.

Returning to the point made above that many of the facilities for retreat are operated by members of the Roman Catholic orders, it is worthwhile to spend a few minutes discussing the need to be both flexible and tactful while being their guests. For many Protestants with no background in the Roman Catholic tradition, many of the practices—the wearing of special clothes, the practice of long periods of silence, the practices of celibacy and poverty, the strong presence of Jesus' mother, Mary, within their Catholic theology, among others—may strike a non-Catholic as misguided at best. Without entering into the theological debate around these matters, it would be best to remember that you are effectively a guest in their home. They have a strong desire to demonstrate the hospitality and love of Christ to you during your stay. They will not be attempting to proselytize to you, nor is this the appropriate forum for you to attempt to do the same to them. It will actually prove more enlightening to enter into dialogue regarding the common heritage that all Christian traditions have. These exchanges will help you to identify the distinctive aspects of your faith, and the practice of articulating them to others will prove a beneficial byproduct of your stay. However, if you believe that you will be stretching your comfort zone already by merely entering in to retreat, make your first endeavor occur at a facility that will more closely align with your particular faith tradition. Although it is possible that you may find one location that is perfect for your own spiritual growth and you will continue to attend there year after year, you should also reserve some time to experience the deep and rich tradition of a Roman Catholic retreat center at some point in your life.

This has been a very practical chapter, trying to answer the initial questions of how long and where to endeavor to partake in a spiritual retreat. In the next chapter we will explore in more detail the question of what to do while in retreat to maximize the potential spiritual growth that you hope to achieve. This will be a discussion of both the practical and the theological. We will explore not only the what of retreat, but the why of these particular activities that we will review.

Chapter 9: Structuring Your Retreat

P resuming you have been convinced of the benefits of retreat and have identified where and when you are going on your retreat, you are now ready to plan the structure and content of your retreat. Much like the discussion on types of spirituality, there are potentially three approaches to structuring the content of your retreat—classical, New Age, and biblical. But before exploring these three in some detail, we should probably address the question of why we need to have any structured content at all. Why not just "go with the flow" and just see how things progress?

The most practical response to the question would appear to lie in the nature of most human beings. Without some type of structure and direction, most individuals with limited training in a particular area are likely to have a suboptimal result for the time spent in the area. Utilizing another sports analogy, if you enter a workout gymnasium and have no familiarity with the science of exercise and what all the equipment is designed to do, it is unlikely that you will exit the gymnasium in a couple of hours having made the optimal move forward in your efforts to improve your general physical condition. You may be better off for at least entering the gym and trying some of the equipment than if you had just stayed at home watching television, but you may be just as likely to misuse the equipment and pull a muscle or otherwise injure yourself.

Although the analogy breaks down somewhat in the spiritual realm, the comparison is not without some parallels. Entering into retreat with no prescribed approach to your actions is likely to produce some ancillary benefits by just being in the surroundings. Just the opportunity to be away with the acknowledged purpose of seeking to draw closer to God may instinctively lead to more prayer, reading of the Bible, and contemplation of the meaning of life than if you had stayed at home. Still, history has shown us that the practice of certain exercises and disciplines has proven beneficial to retreatants over the years. Again, presuming that many reading this book have not participated in an individual spiritual retreat in the past, providing some guidelines and approaches to structuring your initial retreat only seems appropriate. With that background, let us take a look at the three options mentioned above.

New Age Retreat Practices

This book was prepared for the specific audience of Christians— Protestant Christians in particular. As such, only a cursory review of New Age practices will be outlined, as these practices are not consistent with an individual Christian's desire to use the time away as an opportunity to deepen one's relationship with the triune God of Christendom.

The New Age movement is a Western spiritual movement that developed in the second half of the twentieth century. It draws upon both Eastern and Western spiritual traditions and infuses them with the humanistic influences of self-help, holistic health, parapsychology, alternative consciousness, and elements of quantum physics.[133]

New Age adherents are attempting to create a spirituality that is inclusive and pluralistic and "without borders and confining dogmas."[134] The movement holds to a very holistic view of spirituality, involving all elements of the person as well as elements of science and spirituality. Given this open-ended philosophy on spirituality and the emphasis on the entire being, many of the practices of a New Age retreat would involve quasiphysical activities such as meditative yoga, meditation, holistic medical practices, and other participant-centered activities focused on raising the consciousness of the individual to its ultimate potential.

The focus of such a retreat is on the individual, which would be in total contrast with a Christian-based retreat, where the focus is on our sovereign God. Without further discussion, it should be obvious why participating in such a retreat would be in sharp contrast with someone seeking to engage in a Christian retreat in the traditional or biblical sense.

Classical Retreat Content

Classical retreat content borrows heavily from (or even imitates) the rules or disciplines established by leaders of Roman Catholic orders. In this chapter we will examine in some detail the Spiritual Exercises of Saint Ignatius and the *Rule of Saint Benedict*. Although that is by default a fairly narrow analysis of the content of such retreats, it should provide readers some sense of the organization and structure of lay retreats following a classical framework.

The Spiritual Exercises of Saint Ignatius

We touched upon Saint Ignatius in the prior chapter when discussing potential lengths of retreat. We will now focus on the content and structure of such a retreat format in more detail. Although many books have been written about the Ignatian method or Ignatian spirituality, certain key elements must be present to truly adhere to these principles.

> The exercitant must be active, for passivity is impossible in this type of retreat. Perfect silence must be maintained, or the retreat cannot be called Ignatian, no matter how closely the book of the Exercises is otherwise followed. Constant observance of

the movements of the soul must be practiced by the exercitant, and prayers for grace must be frequent. Moreover, unless the director explains the additions and rules for each week, and stresses the essential movement of the soul from indifference through compunction to devotion to Christ, contemplation of His mysteries, reform of life and union, and familiarity with God, we cannot speak of the retreat as Ignatian.[135]

Also key to the idea of an Ignatian retreat is the use of a retreat master. This is an individual who "has grasped the mind and heart of Ignatian spirituality, which is distinguished [by his] service of Christ."[136] The idea of a retreat master, director, spiritual coach, or other type of counselor has not been discussed in detail up to this point. We will save a more extensive analysis of the role and need for such an individual until later in the chapter. At this point, suffice it to say that the spiritual master in the Ignatian retreat is an individual who is fully cognizant of the various spiritual exercises and can effectively gauge the spiritual maturity of the retreatant and best customize the exercises to the needs of the individual. The design of the Ignatian retreat is not to proceed rigidly and equally through the exercises. Rather, with the direction of the spiritual master, certain exercises are emphasized and others limited or even eliminated. With that in mind, you can see why the classic "thirty-day retreat" may in fact be considerably shorter or even longer than thirty days.

What, then, are these exercises?

This expression "Spiritual Exercises" embraces every method of examination of conscience, of meditations, of contemplation, of vocal and mental prayer, and of other spiritual activity … For just as strolling, walking, and running are bodily exercises, so spiritual exercises are methods of preparing and disposing the soul to free itself of all inordinate attachments, and after accomplishing this, of seeking and discovering the Divine Will regarding the disposition of one's life, thus insuring the salvation of his soul.[137]

In particular, the spiritual exercises are grouped together under a common theme in order for the retreatant to be able to progress in an orderly progression from being a self-centered individual burdened by sin to an individual whose focus in every aspect of life is Christ centered. This requires a series of steps (called "weeks") that move the individual along this growth path to spiritual maturity. The following is a cursory outline of the topics and exercises addressed in each week.[138]

I) First week

    (A) Examination of conscience

        (1) Daily

        (2) In general

        (3) General confession and communion

    (B) The first exercise: identification of sin in your life

    (C) The second exercise: meditation on sin

    (D) The third exercise: repetition of the first and second exercises

    (E) The fourth exercise: contemplation of the third exercise

    (F) The fifth Exercise: a meditation on hell

        (1) Four observations of penance

II) Second week: the kingdom of Christ

    (A) First day contemplations

        (1) The incarnation

        (2) The nativity

        (3) A repetition of the first and second exercises

        (4) Second repetition of the first and second exercises

(5) Application of the senses

(B) Second day: repeat the first day contemplations

(C) Third day: prelude to the consideration of the states of life

(D) Fourth day

    (1) A meditation on two standards

    (2) The three classes of men

(E) Fifth day: contemplation on the departure of Christ of Nazareth

(F) Sixth day: contemplation of Christ in the desert

(G) Seventh day: how Saint Andrew and others followed Christ

(H) Eighth day: the Sermon on the Mount

(I) Ninth day: how Christ appeared to His disciples on the waves of the sea

(J) Tenth day: how our Lord preached in the temple

(K) Eleventh day: the resurrection of Lazarus

(L) Twelfth day: Palm Sunday

(M) The three modes of humility

(N) Consideration of choices made in life

(O) Three occasions when a wise and good choice can be made

(P) Directions on amending and reforming one's life and state

III) Third week

    (A) First day

(1) First contemplation: the journey of Christ from Bethany to Jerusalem

(2) Second contemplation: the Last Supper and the garden

(B) Second day: the events of the passion

(C) Third day: the events of the passion

(D) Fourth day: the events of the passion

(E) Fifth day: the events of the passion

(F) Sixth day: the events of the passion

(G) Seventh day: the entire passion

(H) Rules to be observed in the matter of food

IV) Fourth week

(A) First contemplation

(B) Contemplation to attain divine love

(C) Three methods of prayer

(1) The first method of prayer

(2) The second method of prayer

(3) The third method of prayer

(D) The mysteries of the life of our Lord

Even a cursory review of the outline provides some guidance as to the approach of the Ignatian retreat. An initial focus on one's own sinfulness and the need for a savior prepares the ground for abandoning one's own desires (which lead only to sin) and a strong desire to change one's life. A curriculum of prayer, meditation, and Bible readings on the life of Christ move the retreatant forward in understanding that Christ's example is the way to true spiritual maturity. A pattern of prayer cements our relationship with our God and Savior and invites the Holy Spirit to fill us and use us as God would have us used.

One can see why over the centuries, many have found Ignatian retreats extremely valuable in renewing and refreshing the soul. Elements of prayer, thematic Bible reading, and deep contemplative episodes have potential applicability to any retreatant, and these elements will be reviewed when summarizing the elements of a Bible-based retreat.

Benedict's Way

You may recall from chapter three and the discussion of the emergence of the monastic movement that Saint Benedict established a set of governing principles to guide the daily life of the monks living in community. Certainly of the seventy-three rules he adopted, many do not have direct applicability to the individual undertaking a personal retreat. However, embedded in the structure and routines he established are several elements that have been adopted by Roman Catholics over the years when partaking in personal retreat. Core to the Benedictine way of life are humility, obedience, sacred rhythm, and relationships. These are expressed through service to each other through work and praise and worship of God through prayer and chanting. The *Rules* offer practical insights on how these values can be honored. A structured time on retreat that models the structure of daily Benedictine life can help the individual retreatant make these values real in their daily lives. A cursory review of some of these rules shows how this evolution might occur:[139]

Rule one: listen and attend to the master's heart. The master is someone with superior spiritual understanding. Its role can be filled by a spiritual director, God's word, a well-written book, or the Holy Spirit. The key is to open up your heart and listen attentively for the leading of God toward the path of maturity.

Rule seven: humility is a virtue to be actively sought after. In particular the humility of recognizing our state before the Lord should be reflected upon and engendered in our beings. We must recognize that we are the creatures, not the creators, of this world. Humbling ourselves at all times and especially when in retreat can help us put aside barriers that may keep us from fully hearing what God has to say to us.

Rule nineteen: deep reverence for the Lord should be developed. While many of us can acknowledge with our lips that our God is an awesome God, many times our hearts are not fully convinced. If we could walk away from retreat with only one objective filled, it would be that we could truly know God and honor Him as the Creator worthy of all worship and adoration.

Rule twenty: prayer should be heartfelt and short in nature unless prolonged under the inspiration of divine grace. Conversational prayer punctuated frequently by a time of just listening for God's response should prove more useful than long, rote prayers lacking in true fervency and passion.

Rule thirty-five: service to others around us is an imitation of Christ's behavior. In particular, when you are in the company of others in retreat, take the opportunity to serve. This can take place at mealtime in particular. Avoiding the opportunity to assist someone so that you don't "distract yourself from time with God" is totally missing a key point of Scripture. When we serve others in Christ's name, we are serving Him.

Rules thirty-nine and forty: regulate the timing, type, and quantity of food at meals. Although retreat may be used as a time to practice the spiritual discipline of fasting, it need not be. However, it surely is not a time for meals that are unhealthy or overly large in portions. The time of retreat is a time of worldly simplicity so that a temporary separation of the daily routine can be accomplished and a singular focus on the Lord can occur. Sumptuous dining can only serve as a distraction from the real task at hand.

Rule forty-two: enjoy the opportunity to read edifying books, especially during quiet times after dinner. There is much that can be learned by reviewing the classic spiritual books. These books have stood the test of time, and their messages are as relevant today as when they were written. Take advantage of the time at the end of the day to fill your mind with material that will assist you in the deepening of your relationship with your Father.

Rule forty-eight: daily manual labor should occur even when on retreat. Long periods of idleness, even when in prayer, contemplation, or sacred reading, can prove unproductive when the body is not attentive due to pent-up energy or impatience. Interspersing periods of physical activity with periods of rest will often prove more effective than marathon sessions of sedentary reflection.

There are potentially several more areas where the *Rules of Saint Benedict* can provide us with insights on the content and structure of individual retreat. Even this simple list can certainly shed light on why the *Rules* have been the standard for monastic community conduct for nearly 1,500 years and why they still have applicability to Christians of all denominations even today.

Just as we discovered when discussing classical spirituality earlier in the book, the classic traditions, although not all fully applicable to the modern Protestant, certainly can provide some guidance and a starting point for designing one's individual retreat. With this in mind, let us take a look at the potential structure of an individual retreat from the biblical perspective.

Biblical Retreat Content

The admonition in Mark 12:30 to love the Lord with your whole heart, soul, mind, and strength can serve as the framework for constructing a biblically based personal retreat. A retreat based on these principles will involve the whole person. It will be a retreat that seeks to make a connection with all that you are as a person created in His image.

When Mark recorded this quotation of Christ quoting Deuteronomy 6:4, the point was that we are to love God with every aspect of our being. In fact, to emphasize this point, Christ added the word *mind* to the original quotation to account for the fact that to the Hellenized Jews, the mind was a distinct element not separately conceived prior to the influence of Greece. To the Old Testament Jew, these categories were not separate compartments, nor did the terms have even the same precise meaning as they would to a Western Christian today. However, using the definitions that will resonate with today's believer, we will examine these elements of who were are and how they can relate to our Savior. With this framework in mind, let us look at ways we can involve our hearts, souls, minds, and strength in a structured way during a period of personal retreat.

The Heart

When examining the concept of the heart, we are speaking of the emotional side of who we are. Recognizing that God has given everyone a unique personality, what can be an emotional moment or response for one individual may not be such for another. Some individuals are created to strongly react to a potentially emotional episode with a euphoric outburst. Others will barely lift an eyebrow. The individual outward reaction is not the critical issue. The issue is that by loving God with your whole heart you feel internally the emotion of true love. The desire to know and be known by God at an emotional level reflects true commitment to your relationship with your heavenly Father. What types of activities engender this type of deep down connectivity? Many of the same ones that engender this type of relationship at a human level—time together, serious discussions, the knowledge that the other person in fact loves you, and a commitment to a relationship that is enduring—can do so.

The spiritual retreat is one such format for spending focused amounts of time together in deep discussion. When we are not in a hurry and stressed by everyday activities, we can spend significant amounts of time in prayer. We can ask the Lord to reveal Himself to us. We can openly reflect on what issues regarding our relationship we still have questions about, and we can wait upon the Lord for answers only He can give. We can spend time in God's Word reflecting on our own unfaithfulness to the relationship and God's provision of His Son as the great reconciler. As probably the most well-known verse in the Bible says, "For God so loved the world, that he gave his only Son, that whoever believes in him should not perish but have eternal life."[140] Our time in retreat is just one step toward confirming to Him that we are serious about having a relationship that does not fade, but is enduring and everlasting.

Soul

Of the four ways we are to love God, the soul is perhaps the one aspect of our humanity that is the most difficult to define and act upon. Even before the time of Christ, the ancient philosophers struggled to describe what it was that made humans different from every other living creature. Aristotle called it the "first actuality" of a naturally organized body.[141] Plato and Socrates considered the soul "the essence" that made a man who he was. Thomas Aquinas also defined the soul as the first actuality, the thing that gave us our spiritual nature. It was not housed in any organ and as such it would continue to live after our bodies had died.[142] Without delving further, Christians have come to know the soul as the eternal part of us that makes us creatures created in the image of God. It is our souls that make us truly human and hold the essence of our eternal life. If the heart is the seed of our emotional existence, the soul is the seed of our spiritual nature.

So how do you incorporate exercises during your retreat that will speak to the soul? We have some clues given to us by observing how the word *soul* is contextualized in Scripture. The word *soul* is used more in the book of Psalms than in any other book of the Bible, appearing in fifty-five of the 150 Psalms. In many of those Psalms the word *soul* is used multiple times. In the vast majority of these cases the Psalms are Psalms of praise. During times of retreat when we are focusing on the heart, we will be prone to silent, intimate prayer expressing our love for God. During times of retreat when we are honoring the soul, we can think of these exercises as being vocal, worshiping times. We are now connecting with God at the deepest spiritual level. This is engendered by reaching out to our God with songs and Psalms of worship and praise. At this point, our spiritual nature is most open to connecting with the spiritual nature of our Creator.

Mind

As indicated above, the word *mind* was recorded by Mark when Jesus was responding to the scribe who asked him, "Which commandment is most important?" This change was meant to capture the fact that between the Old and New Testaments, Alexander the Great had spread Greek culture throughout the known world. The Greeks valued the mind and viewed it as a separate organ with distinct functions from the heart and soul. To ensure that the reader understood that this command was really a command to love God with every part of ourselves, the word *mind* was added. This is also particularly relevant to someone in today's Western culture. We have been inculcated to believe that religion is a personal and emotional thing. This could not be further from the truth. Our religion is one of faith, but it is a faith born of reason and logic. There have been many excellent books written on how we are to be "thinking Christians," so that point won't be discussed in detail now. Suffice it to say that when we participate in retreat, our minds should be an active part of the exercises that we do.

One way to exercise the mind for the glory of God is to spend time in retreat delving in to the history and theology of our Christian faith. There are numerous excellent resources to choose from. In addition, most retreat centers have libraries of books for you to utilize. The key is that whatever you select should be challenging. It should deal with some aspect of theology, church history, or Christian worldview. This is not the time to sit and read Christian self-help books. As a general rule, reserve this time for one of the recognized "Christian classics." If the book has been published in the last one hundred years, it has not yet stood the test of time to be considered a classic. Spend your time on retreat growing your mind and loving and knowing the Lord with the best books possible. Appendix A provides a list of one hundred books that the author believes are worth the time to take and read on retreat.

Strength

Loving the Lord with all your strength can be thought of in multiple dimensions. Certainly, those who have grown up in America think of strength in terms of physical strength. This is a kind of "brute strength" that we have come to admire in our athletes or cinema action heroes. This type of strength would not appear to have a lot of applicability to the retreat setting. However, even in the retreat setting, the idea of physicality does have a role. As we discussed earlier in this chapter, Benedict required all of those trying to follow his way to work a minimum of five hours every day. Physical labor has a role in retreat. By walking the grounds, hiking through adjacent territories, helping with the gardens, or doing any number of other tasks, we are exercising our bodies, which are gifts of God. We might also be exercising the privilege of service to others. We can also incorporate prayer time and contemplation within these periods of exercise. God gave us our bodies—and they are truly marvelous in their construction. We honor God by taking care of them and using them to help those in need.

Loving God with all our strength also has the connotation of loving God as deeply and intently as possible. When following the other spiritual disciplines of prayer, contemplation, study, Bible reading, reflection, and any other exercise, do it with as much focus and intensity as possible. You are at a retreat for only a fixed period of time. Stay focused, stay intent, and love Him with all the strength you can muster.

Using the above as an outline, in the next chapter we will look at some suggested formats for one-day, three-day, and seven-day retreats. Before looking in detail at these potential retreat structures, we will return to look at one additional item that has been mentioned before but not fully discussed: the use of a spiritual director or coach.

Use of Spiritual Director

In the past couple of chapters, we have alluded to the concept of a spiritual director. For the purposes of this discussion, the terms *spiritual coach*, *director*, and *guide* will be used interchangeably. There can be subtle differences between these roles, but the subtlety at this level of introductory discussion is not warranted. For the purposes of this discussion, the spiritual guide is an individual who will accompany you on your retreat (or potentially someone who is resident at the retreat center) and provide guidance on the spiritual exercises and direction on how to maximize the benefits of the retreat. Again, utilizing the sports analogy, the spiritual coach is someone who is experienced in the methods and practices of retreat and can assist someone who is relatively new to the experience of retreat. They can provide structure, advice, and feedback during the period of retreat.

This person is not a counselor in the sense that he or she has received training and accreditation in the field of Christian or secular counseling. That does not mean that such individuals could not also be spiritual guides. Given the potentially short-term and focused nature of an individual retreat, this would not be the same role as someone who meets regularly over an extended period of time to deal with difficult issues in an individual's life. Part of the reason for making this statement is to remove the stigma that results from the comparison of the retreat guide to a counselor in response to those individuals who might be quick to say, "But I don't need a counselor!"

This person is not necessarily the same as a mentor in that again the role of guide may be for just this specific period of retreat. It is possible that, should an individual continue periodic retreats over several years and always have the use of the same director, the role of mentor might be created. When that happens, that should be considered a bonus.

What the spiritual director can do is provide a sounding board for a thoughtful construction of the exercises and disciplines to be undertaken during a period of retreat. By discussing with the director in what areas the retreatant is feeling particular in need of focus, the two of them can construct an appropriate curriculum. By being on-site during the retreat, the guide can also be available to discuss some of the lessons being learned during the day and suggest adjustments to the content of the remainder of the retreat if needed. Relying on the training and experience that the coach has received, he or she can offer sage advice that can certainly be most beneficial, in particular for the new retreatant.

The best spiritual directors do not attempt to impose their own particular methods of retreat on another individual. Rather, they come alongside the individual who has undertaken the pilgrimage and give general guidance to ensure that the retreatant moves forward on the path to spiritual maturity. They listen and offer suggestions but are never condescending or dictatorial. They are also quick to acknowledge that they do not have all the answers and that they themselves are still learning. It is certainly possible that the individual retreatant may come to the point of their initial retreat with more background in theology than the guide. The retreatant should look upon the coach as an available resource who has only his or her best interests at heart.

With the above discussion, it may appear that the question, "Do I need an individual spiritual guide in order to have a fruitful period of retreat?" has been answered with a definite yes. In reality, the answer is a definite maybe. A well-qualified, trained, and experienced spiritual director can assist anyone going on retreat. The degree to which someone interacts and meets with his or her guide during retreat can vary significantly. The novice retreater can learn much from spending several hours with their guide over the course of a three-day retreat. The experienced retreatant may have more limited interaction, and the time spent together may be more in the nature of peer-to-peer discussion. The key is finding an individual who is a good match for you in terms of temperament and whom you feel comfortable dialoguing with at a genuine level. Whether this individual is someone who is resident at the retreat house or someone who has elected to accompany you on the retreat is not as critical as it being the right person.

For those individuals who elect not to use a formalized version of a spiritual coach, there is still tremendous value to be achieved from going on retreat. There are certainly resources available to help you think through the most effective way to structure your retreat. Certainly, just reading and contemplating the Bible could be more than sufficient. After all, the person we are really attempting to connect more intimately with is Jesus Christ, who is ultimately everyone's best option as a spiritual coach.

Chapter 10: Example of Retreat Content

With the background and structure provided by the prior chapter, the following illustrative examples of one-, three- and seven-day retreats are outlined below. These are examples, not prescribed formats. Depending on where the individual retreatant is in his or her spiritual journey will dictate a lot of the specifics of the content of the retreat. These suggested approaches presume that the individual retreatant is a professing Christian with some core theological and Biblical principles already in hand. It does not presume any formalized seminary training, but rather contemplates an individual believer who has taken their faith seriously but recognizes there is still much to learn. These should be pretty safe assumptions, for it is not likely the individual would undertake a personal retreat without most of these characteristics.

Outline of a One-Day Retreat

In chapter eight, we indicated that a one-day retreat is often not sufficient to really undergo the process of fully breaking away from the cares of the day and giving more or less undivided attention to the purpose of a retreat. That being said, there will be occasions where an individual has a twenty-four-hour period available and is seeking the chance to supplement other, longer retreats to be undertaken at other times of the year. These miniretreats—particularly if focused on seeking

God's counsel on one particular issue—can prove most beneficial. For example, let us presume that the individual has been presented with a new job opportunity and is really conflicted about pursuing the position. He has sought advice from family and friends, and they have given the individual a lot to consider, but after several days of seeking advice from others, the person is no closer to reaching a conclusion. With this issue as the singular focus, the following might be a potential structure for a one-day retreat on the topic.

(1) Rise early and pray for thirty minutes. In particular at this point in time, pray specifically for guidance and wisdom. Also pray that distractions are kept at a minimum so you can really focus on the issue at hand. You should also consider journaling briefly during the day after each spiritual exercise about any insights God may give you or any reactions you have to something you read or is revealed to you.

(2) After addressing personal hygiene issues, proceed to breakfast, preferably in silence. With a one-day retreat you might also consider making this a day of fasting. Even if you eat, keep the meal simple.

(3) Locate a quiet place where you are less likely to be distracted. Since your primary focus of the day is wisdom concerning a potential career change, make the focus of your biblical and extrabiblical reading track along the themes of wisdom and vocation. Spend the next hour to ninety minutes reading through the book of Proverbs. Read contemplatively, seeking to absorb every word and stopping to pray after every few chapters, asking God to reveal to you any insights from what you have just read. Update your journal accordingly.

(4) Exercise your body. Take a walk or a bike ride or some other type of activity that will burn off some of the nervous energy and better prepare you for the time ahead when your body may be

sedentary but your soul very active. Depending on your physical condition, the exercise should last thirty to sixty minutes. It should be undertaken in silence, although you should be in frequent conversation with the Lord, reviewing the issue of the day and asking Him how to identify the pros and cons of each alternative.

(5) You should pre select one of the spiritual classics that can give perspective on the issue of the day—perhaps excerpts from *The Practice of the Presence of God* by Brother Lawrence, who spent most of his life as a cook in a monastery kitchen. This may help give perspective on the need for a life (including our secular vocation) that is focused on acknowledging God in everything that we do and in every moment of our lives. Read the selected book during available gaps in your schedule.

(6) Break for lunch (or not, depending on whether you are intending to fast) in silence. Again, the meal should be simple and not particularly time-consuming to make or eat.

(7) Spend time in concentrated and consecrated prayer. You may want to focus on one or two particular aspects of God, such as Yahweh the Provider (Jehovah-Jireh) or God our Shepherd. After an appropriate amount of time just acknowledging God's holiness and awesomeness, bring to Him the particulars or your conundrum and open your heart to His input. Continue this for as long as you feel God providing insights. Enter into deep dialogue with the holy counselor. At the end of this time in prayer, spend sufficient time recording any additional observations you now have.

(8) At the conclusion of this time in prayer, renew yourself physically with another walk. This time, try to be in a place where you can see the majesty of His creation. Walk in the woods or on a shoreline. Spend time just marveling at the power of our almighty God. This should be a period of renewal after some intense time of serious reflection.

(9) Return once again to the Scriptures. Use a concordance and look up Scriptures of key words that define the issue you are struggling with. In this case you might look up the passages that use the words *work* or *money*. Again, record any observations that you have.

(10) Depending on the time of day, you can either break for dinner, or if you still have time, return once again to reading from the spiritual classic you have selected and then have dinner. Again, you still have work in front of you. Make the meal nourishing, but not overly filling. If you have elected to use a spiritual director, this might be an appropriate time to sit with them and discuss your observations of the day and preliminary thoughts on the answer to the question of the day.

(11) Take another short walk and allow your food to settle. Depending on the time of year, you may want to watch the sunset and thank God for the creation He has provided.

(12) If you did not have time prior to dinner, return to some reading from your spiritual classic. If you did read it prior to dinner, still continue in selected readings, but for a more abbreviated time.

(13) Review your journal of observations made during your day so far. See if a pattern is developing that is beginning to crystalize an answer to your question. Hopefully, by now, a direction of which way you are headed is developing, but honestly assess if there are still some unanswered parts of the inquiry. Spend time in prayer or biblical review seeking to gain further clarity.

(14) Once a potentially final decision is formulated, take your answer to God in prayer. Ask Him to confirm your thoughts. Ask Him to challenge your thinking. Pray for final confirmation on the direction you are to pursue and then pray some more for peace of mind on the decision made.

(15) Go to bed early. You deserve it. This has been a long and demanding day but hopefully one that has also drawn you closer to God and given you the confidence that you are now prepared to proceed as He has guided.

Outline of a Three-Day Retreat

The outlines of the three- and seven-day retreats are not going to be as precise as the above one-day retreat outline. For one thing, it will be hard to keep up the intensity of schedule outlined above for multiple days. It will not be necessary to do that, either, as you will develop a rhythm as you spend more time with the Lord. Structure of some type is still needed to ensure some level of focus, but the specific exercises could certainly be lengthened, shortened, or substituted. For the purposes of the following outlines, there is no presumed agenda other than to know your God in a more intimate and loving way.

Friday

The day's theme is your position before God, your state of mind coming to retreat, what you can put behind you for the weekend, particular issues or sins in your life, and the recognition that you are someone who has failed God but who has been redeemed.

The Day's Activities

(1) Rising early for prayer: focus on your needs and what you hope to accomplish this weekend on retreat. Ask for God's wisdom and guidance through each step.

(2) Breakfast: keep it simple and eat in silence, and take a walk or engage in some other physical exercise after breakfast.

(3) Morning session: read selected passages from both the Old

and New Testaments. Read contemplatively, poring over each passage. Write in a journal of recent events in your life and open prayer requests. Reflect on how this morning's passages have applicability to the items noted in your journal. At some point, take a fifteen-minute break and walk around or stretch.

(4) Morning physical time: take a long walk or bike ride. Feel free to listen to worship songs on a mobile device if it can be done safely.

(5) Lunch: keep it simple and eat in silence.

(6) Afternoon reading time: preselect a book on a spiritual issue, either a recognized spiritual classic or a book that has been highly recommended to you from a knowledgeable source. The goal is to complete the book in five one-hour sittings over the next three days. By default, the book will likely be two hundred pages or less.

(7) Afternoon prayer time: Friday is the day of cleansing and confession. Identify areas in your life that you believe are areas of weakness in your spiritual walk. Raise these areas up one at a time to the Lord, acknowledging your desire for His help and asking for the intervention of the Holy Spirit to strengthen you in times of weakness. Spend time reading through the crucifixion account in a couple of different Gospels. Reflect on the great love of God the Father and the great obedience of God the Son in sacrificing for sinful mankind.

(8) Afternoon physical time: take a short walk or do some other type of exercise (or help with a work project if available on-site).

(9) Rest for a short while before dinner.

(10) Dinner: partake in dinner. Communication with other retreatants, your spiritual guide, or the host of the retreat center is encouraged. Dinner should be simple, but substantive.

(11) Daily journal: plan on keeping a daily journal of your time in retreat. You can make quick notes during the day, but set aside thirty minutes in the evening after dinner to organize the notes and record a more cohesive summary of the day's experiences and lessons for future review and reflection.

(12) Spend a second hour reading from your selected book.

(13) Spend some personal time listening to a recorded lecture or just relaxing and conversing.

(14) Evening prayers: reflect again upon today and prepare yourself for Saturday. Pray in particular for those family members you may have left behind that things are well on the home front. Focus once again on God's plan of salvation and the incredible sacrifice of Christ on the cross.

(15) Bedtime

Saturday

The focus of the day is on growing spiritually, being aware of God's desire that we know him and love him as He loves us, attempting to ingrain in our lives an eternal perspective, and seeking God's wisdom and guidance as we offer up every action to him in praise.

(1) Arise early: offer the day to the Lord in prayer. Ask Him to guide your every step today. Ask Him to open your eyes and your heart so that you seek to honor Him with your every action.

(2) Bible reading: select passages from both the Old and New Testaments. As you read them, ask how these passages tell the story of salvation. Although you are reading for comprehension, at this time you are not in a contemplative reading mode.

(3) Breakfast: keep it simple and relatively plain. You might also consider making Saturday your fast day (or at least eight hours of the day), but this is certainly not required.

(4) Morning physical activity: walk or work or both. The longer the retreat, the more of the day that can be devoted to such activities. On a three-day retreat it would be appropriate to participate in physical activities three hours a day or even a little more. During this period of physical activity your mind and your spirit are still focused on God. These opportunities are great for silent prayer or even reflection on a particular passage of Scripture.

(5) Morning reading time

(6) Lunchtime: maintaining the theme, all the meals should be simple and require minimal preparation and cleanup time. If you are not required to make your meals, volunteer to assist those who are. Attempt to observe a period of silence at this time.

(7) Time of contemplative reading of Scripture: select passages that deal with today's topic of spiritual growth. For example, read through the Sermon on the Mount, noting the characteristics of blessedness and contrast those to what the world would view as blessed.

(8) Afternoon prayers: focus intently on what it means to be a child of God. Ask God to point out to you areas for personal spiritual growth. Ask God to enable you to handle the "meat" of the Word. Ask God to give you an eternal perspective—one where you honor Him in your daily activities but are ever mindful that we are but sojourners in this earthly world.

(9) Afternoon physical activity

(10) Dinner: take time to discuss some of the lessons learned with other retreatants, the staff, or your coach.

(11) Second hour of reading

(12) Journal of the day's activities

(13) Personal time

(14) Evening prayers: ask God to continue to develop you into the believer He would have you be. Also pray for those at home, and pray that God prepare you for your final day of retreat.

(15) Bedtime

Sunday

The theme of the day is joy and celebration for being a child of God. This is the day of resurrection and reconciliation—your focus is on knowing God better and having a thankful heart for having been redeemed.

(1) Early morning prayer: awake and give the day to the Lord. Where Friday was a day of contrition and Saturday a day of maturing, today the focus is on knowing and loving God. Depending on the time of year, if you can be up and looking outside at sunrise, read the Easter morning passages out of two or three of the Gospels.

(2) Breakfast

(3) Partake in Sunday service with others if offered. If not, spend time reading God's Word and praying. Consider singing and offering praise or at least reading some of the Psalms of celebration. Partake in Communion as a group, or, if that is not possible, consider reading the passages of the Last Supper and contemplate as if you were in the room with Jesus Christ and the twelve apostles at this first communion.

(4) Morning physical activity

(5) Final hour of reading

(6) Lunch

(7) Afternoon of contemplative Bible passage reading: consider staying in the praise Psalms or other passages that extol the magnificence of God our Creator

(8) Afternoon time of prayer

(9) Afternoon physical activity

(10) Afternoon journaling

(11) Final preparation to leave

(12) Evening meal and/or departure

Again, this is only a sample outline of how you might structure your three-day weekend retreat. There are certainly multiple variations. However, you can begin to see the pattern that is developing. There is a flow from conversational prayer to Bible study to physical activity to contemplative study and prayer and then to journaling. Hopefully through these exercises you can walk away at the end of the third day with the feeling that you have truly drawn closer to the Lord.

The Seven-Day Retreat

With the pattern created with the three-day retreat, the seven-day retreat can be summarized in a more succinct fashion. For one thing, it would be perfectly acceptable to attach the Friday-through-Sunday activities above on the end of your weeklong retreat. Presuming that to be the case, this section will cover some of the additional activities that should be considered during the week and then give a cursory review of the structure of the Monday-through-Thursday time frame.

Fasting

In particular if a longer period like a seven-day retreat is involved, you should consider a day of fasting as part of your retreat experience. This might be coupled with a daily schedule that has limited physical activity, and in place of that time, consider filling the space with additional time of prayer. Depending on your familiarity and experience in the discipline of fasting, you may limit the actual fasting time from sunrise to sunset. Another option would be to fast from solid foods but drink liquids such as juices and other supplements. You should recognize your own physical limitations. The idea of a fast is not to demonstrate your willingness to suffer, but rather to make you aware of your physical passions and how they might be overemphasized in your life. The desire of the fast is to bring focus and clarity of thought and to instill a dependence on the Lord's provision in your life. It is accompanied by prayer, as the two practices can work in tandem to heighten your time of communication with God. Again, this is a suggestion, certainly not a mandate, but consider it when planning your time away.

One-Day Excursion

The idea of an excursion during a time of extended retreat sounds like an oxymoron. It would be something like advocating taking a one-day vacation while you are on a weeklong vacation stint. However, the idea is that during an extended time of retreat, changing location and routine for a single day can be a way of keeping your retreat effort more productive overall. For example, if your retreat location is in an area that has an historic church or religious site, a visit can prove helpful. By understanding the historic aspects of our faith we can gain an appreciation of our place in the long line of believers who have preceded us and gain more of an appreciation of the development of theological tradition. To worship in an older, historic church can help us gain more of the eternal perspective we are striving for.

If your stay puts you in the vicinity of a Christian college or university, spending some time at the campus chapel or walking the grounds can also serve a similar purpose as a visit to an historical site. You might even consider sitting in on a class in church history, theology, or Christian worldview to broaden your understanding in these key areas of faith.

If you are near a major metropolitan area, you might consider a trip to an art museum where you can review much of Scripture captured in the works of some of the master painters. Again, the historical perspective of Christian worldview can often be traced as one proceeds through the centuries in art. In an alternative to a visit to an art museum as an observer, you might consider a more active role by attempting to create some religious art of your own at a local studio. The options are numerous.

The real meaning of the excursion is not to provide a "break" from your time of retreat. It is to just provide a different forum for renewing yourself spiritually and mentally. The above examples are not exhaustive by any means. The key when incorporating such an activity is that the activity be something that draws you closer to God and your faith. A clothes-shopping experience would not be appropriate, nor would any other activity where the primary focus was on you. Absent violating this rule, many activities are in bounds.

Extended Physical Activity

A day of fasting and prayer can fuel the desire to love the Lord God with your whole heart. Spending time reviewing and reflecting on sacred art, music, or architecture can fuel the soul to love God more deeply. Time spent in a classroom or a lecture or a bookstore will hopefully expand your mind as a vehicle of worship. The strength portion of the formula of loving God should not be ignored during your extended retreat. We had previously discussed that even one- and three-day excursions should allow some time for contemplative walking or other exercises.

When you have set aside a whole week, the opportunity exists for an extended period of physical activity that can be beneficial to your soul as well as your body.

How extensive a period of physical exertion is dictated by the individual's general state of physical wellness. An active twenty-something may be capable of embarking on a ten-kilometer run through the country. A sixty-year-old, even one who has taken care of him- or herself, may have to be reconciled to a ten-kilometer bike ride. The point is to partake in some type of outdoor activity that is strenuous without being potentially damaging to your body. The release of endorphins as well as the ability to burn off excess energy will hopefully promote your becoming more focused and relaxed during your periods of limited physical activity, such as times of prayer and meditation.

This period of physical activity could also include kayaking or canoeing down a river or around a lake, hiking up a hillside, or riding a bike. The key is to use this period of activity as a time for prayer or contemplation. Offer up this period of exertion to God. Think about the wonder of the human body that He has made and give thanks to Him for giving life to you. Your body is a creation of the Lord's for which you are a steward, just like money or any other possession. By connecting your physical well-being to your body as a tool to accomplish God's will in this world, you will hopefully develop a lifestyle that is conducive to honoring God and thanking Him for this great gift.

Service

You might also consider a period a service to others as a part of your retreat. Volunteer to tend the garden or help with chores around the retreat center. You might coordinate in advance a service project in a local community, such as working on the house or yard of someone who is sick or elderly. You can volunteer to serve meals at a local shelter house or to visit the elderly in a nursing home. Again, the opportunities are limitless. By incorporating a period of service within your extended retreat, you are confirming your love for God.

As John wrote in 1 John 4:19–21, "We love because he first loved us. If anyone says, 'I love God' and hates his brother, he is a liar; for he who does not love his brother whom he has seen cannot loved God whom he has not seen. And this commandment we have from him: whoever loves God must also love his brother."

Day One of a Seven-Day Retreat

The theme of the day is loving God with your whole heart.

Recognizing that ethereal, omnipotent and omniscient beings may in fact be difficult to feel love for, the focus of the day is trying to create an environment where you really feel the presence of the Lord in your life. In our human condition, it is very difficult to feel genuine love in our heart for someone we do not feel like we really know on a personal basis. An individual may have great admiration and respect for President Abraham Lincoln. But it would be difficult to state that you love the former president. Living 150 years after his death, with no opportunity to really meet and know him, we cannot create the human emotion of love at the deepest level of our hearts.

With Jesus Christ we have an individual who died but, unlike Abraham Lincoln, rose again and is very much alive today. Although not an individual who can be touched in the physical sense, we should spend time during the day reading biblical passages and contemplating Jesus' perfect humanity. Loving someone with your whole heart reflects a type of intimacy that cannot be achieved with strangers. Spend time journaling and reflecting on the characteristics of God the Father. Deepen your understanding of the nature of the triune God by addressing the prayers of the day toward deepening your relationship with Him. Foster a true love for the God who first loved us even as His rebellious creation.

Consider taking some of the time for a study of the word *heart* as discussed in Scripture. Look in particular for those verses that give us guidance as to a heart that is attentive to God as well as those that discuss a heart hardened toward God. Spend some time assessing your "heart condition."

This might be a day where you carve out some time to serve others. This can help set the tone for the week as someone who is willing to humble him- or herself and be teachable. In addition, this will help cement the idea of demonstrating love for God by loving others created in His image as He commanded.

Day Two of a Seven-Day Retreat

The theme of the day is loving God with your whole soul. When one loves the Lord with one's whole soul, that person is loving God with every emotion and will and fabric of his or her being. Our souls are what make us distinctive from the rest of God's creation and create the special bond between the Creator and His creation. When we love God with our souls, we order our lives in such a way that we create what Augustine called "ordinate love." We so love God that we strive to love the things God loves most. Likewise, we strive to hate the things that God hates. By structuring our lives in such a way, we are following the example of Christ and leading lives that are pleasing to God. We are learning to love God without equal in our lives.

Loving God with our soul can best be demonstrated by obedience to his ordinances. In Luke 14:26–27 Jesus sets the standards for the cost of discipleship when he says, "If anyone comes to me and does not hate his own father and mother and wife and children and brothers and sisters, yes and even his own life, he cannot be my disciple. Whoever does not bear his own cross, and come after me cannot be my disciple."

Christ is not literally telling us to hate our family and ourselves. He is saying that our love of God should be so deep and passionate that when compared to the human love of a family member, it will seem as if we hate them. These twin themes of obedience to God's Word and deep-seated love will guide the activities of this second day.

The theme of your prayer activity should be for God to strengthen you to better do His will in this world. If you are having an area of persistent sin in your life, this would be the time to pray that God helps you overcome it. The Bible passages that you read and meditate upon should focus on God's call to be disciples. Utilize a concordance and do word studies on *obedience, discipleship,* and *soul.* You might consider reading passages from Dietrich Bonhoeffer's *The Cost of Discipleship* or William Law's *A Serious Call to a Devout and Holy Life.*

This might be the appropriate day to plan a trip to an art museum or to attend a concert containing works of Bach or Handel that were composed to praise God. For many individuals, the arts, in particular music, can affect us on the deepest of levels. If a live concert is not available, consider listening to a recorded session. Reflect on the mood of the music, and if so moved, offer up in song your praise to our Father.

Day Three Of A Seven-Day Retreat

The theme of the day is loving the Lord with all your mind. Modern society would have us believe that belief in God is a matter of personal preference. After all, the logic goes, since the existence of God cannot be proven in a scientific manner, it is relegated to the status of an emotional decision. If you accept this faulty logic, then the idea of loving God with your mind seems counterintuitive. After all, if acceptance of a divine creator is an emotional decision, it would seem that loving him with your heart and soul is appropriate—but the mind?

It is no coincidence that some of the most brilliant minds of all time— men such as Blaise Pascal, Isaac Newton, Isaac Milner, and C. S. Lewis— were devoted Christians and defenders of the faith. Following the path of faithfulness to your Christian beliefs does not require abandoning reason and thought. In fact, examining your beliefs under the discerning critique of logic can strengthen your faith immensely. God made us creatures of intellect and reasoning. To ignore this element of your human nature when attempting to grow in our faith will result in a less than optimal result.

Your prayer time during this day should be focused on asking God to give you wisdom, understanding, and knowledge to lead your Christian life in a more fulfilling way. Your Scripture studies for the day can draw from the wisdom literature of the Bible—in particular Proverbs. You might consider reading C. S. Lewis's *Mere Christianity* or some other segments of classic apologetic literature.

This could be an appropriate day to carve some time out to spend reading a book on theology or perhaps attending a lecture that can expand your understanding of the Bible. The purpose of the day is not to make you smarter or better able to respond to questions about your faith (although both of these will hopefully result). The purpose is for you to build up your mind as a tool of worship of the Lord. The exercises undertaken will also solidify your faith by having you address any lingering questions you might have. The only question that cannot be answered is the one never asked. By the end of the day, you should go to bed comforted by the fact that your faith is a reasoned faith and that God gave you a mind to use in His service.

Day Four of a Seven-Day Retreat

The theme of the day is loving the Lord with your whole strength. Americans in particular have always admired gross strength. Heavyweight boxers and weightlifters always seem to draw the larger audiences, even if pound for pound the smaller athletes are much stronger. The physicality of American football has made it America's sport. As Americans we can more readily identify with Samson as a biblical hero then we can Elijah.

Although the body as a gift of God has been discussed in this book and taking time during retreat for physical exercise has been strongly endorsed, this is only one element of what God means when He commands us to love Him with our whole strength. If we treat our bodies as a gift requiring our stewardship, then this will hopefully result in better endurance and stamina that will enable us to focus for a longer time in this world of doing His will. However, loving God with all of your strength as at least a couple of other connotations. When you love God with your whole strength you are acknowledging that you are willing to pay the price of hardships that come from openly demonstrating your faith to a disbelieving world. You are also acknowledging that once you made a commitment of faith, you do not intend to ever turn back to a life marked by earlier sin habits.

Your prayer time today should focus on asking God to strengthen you so that you will be willing to pay the price when called upon. You will also ask Him to fortify you so that your path is forward to Christian maturity with minimal lapses. When selecting Bible passages for study, you might consider the book of Acts, with a particular emphasis on the actions of Paul and Peter on holding fast to the gospel message. Your classic readings for the day might include *Fox's Book of Martyrs* or reading a biographical sketch of individuals who stood strong in their faith and impacted the world, such as William Wilberforce.

This might also be the day to incorporate your extended physical activity. Although loving God with all your strength is certainly not strictly a physical activity, there is a need to care for yourself so that you can be about your Father's business.

Days Five through Seven

As alluded to earlier, you should consider incorporating the activities and focus of the three-day retreat as the concluding framework for your weeklong time of personal retreat. Focusing on the death and resurrection of Christ can solidify the essence of what it means to be a follower of Christ. By examining your position before God and truly asking God to help you grow spiritually your time will be well spent on days five and six. Having the seventh day as a day of celebration and renewal seems particularly appropriate. Those who know Jesus Christ as their personal Savior should be people of joy, and the time you have spent over the last week deepening your relationship should leave you feeling refreshed, renewed, and rededicated.

The end of any retreat period can be a time of mixed emotions. On one hand, you should have a feeling of contentment, as you have spent personal time growing in your faith. You also should come away ready to lead your life every day with the eternal perspective that knowing your God brings. However, you cannot ignore the genuine concern that once you leave the sheltered walls of the retreat center the "reality" of life will hit you head on. You will return to work in the real world and deal with the almost constant bombardment of activities that seemed designed to pull you away from practicing your faith with a renewed vigor. The next chapter will look at some of these issues that will pull you back toward a spiritual malaise and discuss how the spirit of retreat can be kept alive year round.

Chapter 11: How Can I Keep the Spirit of Retreat Alive?

T he practice of spiritual retreat is essential for the maturing of the individual Christian. However, just like the physical renewal you receive from your annual vacation seems to quickly fade once you return to work, you need to guard against the benefits of an annual personal retreat becoming lost in the daily business of life. In short, you need to keep the spirit of retreat alive throughout the year.

What causes this degradation of the value of retreat? There are many reasons, not the least of which are those that we reviewed in chapter one that keep Christians in general from truly living the mature Christian life. The pull of culture in general and today's culture of entertainment in particular robs us of precious time we could be spending in communion with God or serving the needs of His flock. Certainly the human nature of fear, shame, and boredom can weigh us down and cause us to deny some of the life-changing experiences we have on retreat once we return home and to our daily routine. The greatest cause of the falling away from our spiritual practices is the grave problem of sin in our lives. If we let our guard down for even a short while, Satan would love nothing better than for us to backtrack into the malaise of spiritual indifference that we briefly escaped during our period of retreat. So how can we avoid this happening? We will spend this chapter taking a look at ways to combat this very natural regression that can happen if we are not careful.

Discipline

In chapter six we reviewed several spiritual practices that have been adopted by generations of Christians to further their spiritual development. It is no coincidence that these practices have been called spiritual disciplines. The idea of leading a disciplined life is not particularly in vogue with a culture that views flexibility and freedom of choice as key indicators of a liberated lifestyle. Even as followers of Jesus Christ, individuals may shy away from the idea of "discipline" in their life because of the negative connotation of the word. After all, aren't children disciplined because they have done something bad? Who would actually ask for discipline in their lives?

In reality, this negative view is a function of not fully understanding what is meant by the term *discipline* when it is used in the Bible. The Greek word *paideia* is translated as *discipline*. Although it does stand for the idea of chastisement, it also can mean exhortation. *Paideia* is drawn from the root word for child (*pais*) because of the instruction, education, and correction needed to raise a child from youth to adulthood. The Lord, as a loving parent, brings situations into our lives that are meant to have us grow to spiritual maturity. Hebrews 12:5–11 tells us:

> My son, do not regard lightly the discipline of the Lord, nor be weary when reproved by him, for the Lord disciplines the one he loves, and chastises every son whom he receives [quoting Proverbs 3:11–12]. It is for discipline that you have to endure. God is treating you as sons. For what son is there whom his father does not discipline. If you are left without discipline, in which all have participated, then you are illegitimate children and not sons. Besides this, we have had earthly fathers who disciplined us and we respected them. Shall we not much more be subject to the Father of spirits and live? For they disciplined us for short time as it seemed best to them, but he disciplines us for our good, that we may share in his holiness. For the moment all discipline seems painful rather than pleasant, but later it yields the peaceful fruit of righteousness to those who have been trained in it.

Although in the context of the entire book of Hebrews, this verse is dealing with the type of discipline that evidenced itself in the endurance of persecution by the early Christians, the same principles can apply to self-discipline applied in the life of an individual Christian today. Exercising the discipline of fasting or prayer or contemplative reading, even when we have no desire to do so in an earthly sense, can prove a time of growth and encouragement in our lives.

Referring again to the sports analogy of weight lifting, you only strengthen your muscles by first tearing them down under the duress of exercising and then allowing the muscle fibers to grow back stronger. This process of tearing down and rebuilding requires an ever greater commitment in order to continue to progress. Once you can easily handle a certain weight, your forward progress will retard. Only by increasing the weight, the repetitions, or both will you grow stronger. Growth requires resistance in both our physical lives as well as our spiritual ones. When you stop applying resistance, you will stop growing.

When the spiritual retreat practices of Ignatius were reviewed, it was noted there is a high degree of structure to the thirty-day retreat. This structure provides a framework and direction that takes most of the human judgment out of picture. The retreatant follows the spiritual practices not initially out of any strong desire to do so, but rather out of the discipline to improve his or her spiritual walk.

The principle of practicing the spiritual disciplines on a daily basis is one that can keep the spirit of retreat alive in your life. Certainly the intensity and focus of time cannot be as lengthy as at a retreat center, but with discipline, time can be carved out to fruitfully engage in the spiritual practices discussed in chapter six. By incorporating these practices on a monthly or weekly cycle, you ingrain them as habits into your daily life.

C. S. Lewis had an interesting observation regarding the habit of spiritual disciplines in his book *Letters to Malcolm: Chiefly on Prayer*:

> If we were perfected, prayer would not be a duty, it would be a delight. Someday, please God, it will be. The same is true of many other behaviors which now appear as duties. If I loved

my neighbor as myself, most of the actions which are now my moral duty would flow out of me as spontaneously as song from a lark or fragrance from a flower. Why is this not so yet? Well, we know, don't we? Aristotle has taught us that delight is the "bloom" on an unimpeded activity. But the very activities for which we were created are, while we live on earth, variously impeded: by evil in ourselves or in others. Not to practice them is to abandon our humanity. To practice them spontaneously and delightfully is not yet possible. This situation creates the category of duty, the whole specifically moral realm.[143]

Lewis makes the very practical point that good intentions alone are usually not sufficient to achieve good results. The fallen condition of our human nature keeps us from always doing what is best for us. Duty and discipline help us overcome the obstacles in our lives that keep us from attending to what is important in life.

The Bible makes it clear that if we truly love God, we will obey and follow Him. First John 5:2–3 tells us, "By this we know that we love the children of God, when we love God and obey his commandments. For this is the love of God that we keep his commandments and his commandments are not burdensome." All other outward forms of love of God mean very little if we do not keep His commandments. If we struggle to keep His commandments out of pure love, then we should attempt to keep them out of sheer obedience.

This does not mean that the practice of spiritual disciplines will always be more of a chore than a joy. To the contrary, as we spend more and more time drawing closer to God in the practice of the spiritual disciplines, they become at first a habit and then an anticipated joy in our lives. Set up a consistent time of prayer and Bible reading in your daily schedule. Practice fasting on a fixed day of the month (or week). Volunteer your time consistently to assist with an outreach to the poor and needy in your community. What at first will feel like drudgery will give way to a joyful expression of your love of Jesus Christ.

In 1831 an aristocratic Frenchman named Alexis de Tocqueville came to the United States to study the American way of life and its political institutions. He eventually accumulated his observations in a two-volume set focused on the democratic principles of America. He was particularly intrigued by the order and prosperity of the country, despite its extreme individualism. He pondered how such a seeming contradiction could exist. He eventually concluded that it was not a function of the government or the laws it created, but rather the mores of the nation, the moral habits of the heart. He stated, "When the habits of a nation are as they should be, a society of people has much liberty and freedom. For Americans, the ideas of Christianity and liberty are so completely mingled that it is almost impossible to get them to conceive of one without the other."[144]

Many in America would argue that the ideas of Christianity and liberty have become delinked in America today. As such, liberty without moral standards leads to degradation and chaos. The "habits of the heart" that de Tocqueville so admired nearly two hundred years ago have arguably been lost by many Christians as well. Recapturing these habits of heart through regular practice of the spiritual disciplines can keep the fire of personal retreat burning throughout the year.

Accountability

Proverbs 27:17 tells us that "Iron sharpens iron, and one man sharpens another." Of course that reality depends upon the angle of how iron hits iron. When it occurs at the correct angle, the interaction between the two pieces of metal can sharpen iron. Iron can also dull iron when it strikes at the wrong angle. So it is with relationships. Some individuals you interact with can challenge and encourage you and bring out the best in you. Other individuals can prove toxic to your growth. They are draining and discouraging. One way to ensure that you continue to grow between periods of retreat is to associate with individuals who will hold you accountable to a path of spiritual enrichment.

This can be a particularly effective way to avoid backsliding if the individual who is your accountability partner is someone who has attended retreats with you and is familiar with the areas you focused on during retreat. Up until this point in the book, we have treated retreat as a solitary activity. In fact, large portions of the time in retreat are best done with some degree of isolation. The primary focus during spiritual retreats is individual spiritual development. The primary participants are you and God. However, there is certainly nothing wrong with having a companion when you go on retreat. You should just be selective regarding when and how you spend your time together. Meeting once or twice during the day—maybe over meals—can serve as a point to share what each has been learning. This background will obviously help when you meet periodically after the retreat.

Whomever you select to be your accountability partner should be someone for whom you have a high degree of respect and with whom you can share honestly what is happening in your life. One practice that is particularly effective is to share areas where you are prone to difficulty in your spiritual walk with your partner. Each meeting can begin with a series of questions, beginning with "How are you doing in your struggle with …?" The last question in the series should be "Have you been honest in how you have answered the prior questions?" This level of openness requires a high degree of confidentiality and honesty. For those reasons, choose your accountability partner carefully.

Things that should be considered in selecting your partner include the following.

(1) Is your partner at least your equal from a spiritual development perspective? The accountability partner is there to be additive to your spiritual growth. They should have the life experiences and biblical knowledge to see that you are not straying from the path. Their advice should be well grounded in God's Word. We introduced the idea of a spiritual mentor or coach in chapter ten. This individual would not have to fulfill that role during a time of retreat, but should have many of the same characteristics

as a spiritual guide. There should be a depth of character and maturity that leads to a mutual respect. It may be desirable to have the relationship be reciprocal. The mutual accountability ensures that both parties have a vested interest in the success of the relationship.

(2) Are you in geographic proximity to each other? In an age where technology has made face-to-face meetings seem old-fashioned, people may feel that this is less relevant than ever in history. While certainly this is true for a number of recurring relationships, such as in business with customer and vendors, when dealing with the type of deep, personal relationship we are discussing here, live meetings are preferable to other alternatives. Weekly or at least biweekly visits are the suggested frequency of these meetings. With that type of commitment, distance can be a deterrent, so keep location in mind when entering into the accountability partner relationship.

(3) Is this accountability partner relationship a unique relationship? This question is focused on whether or not the two individuals can have other existing relationships such as pastor/member, boss/employee, or even husband/wife. Although no absolute answers exist in this arena, in general, it will probably be healthier if this relationship is unique. Many other relationships, such as those mentioned above, do provide a degree of accountability. However, the spiritual accountability partnership requires an openness to discuss one's faults that may be difficult if another relationship exists between the two individuals.

(4) Are both parties in the position to commit to this relationship? Ideally your accountability partner is in a position where the commitment can be long term. Two or three years would be a minimum time commitment. If one of the parties is subject to frequent job transfers or failing health, the pairing may not be ideal. At the same time, both parties should have the honesty

and freedom to indicate that the partnership is not as effective as was hoped and terminate it without leaving ill will between the two.

Certainly this accountability partner relationship is not the only relationship in a Christian's life that can give guidance regarding spiritual development. For those churches that have small group ministries or discipleship ministries, there exists a network of believers to support an individual. One's spouse can be a very significant influence on how an individual moves forward to spiritual maturity. Perhaps most critical of all is the need for a Christian to be a part of a local body of believers led by a pastor who recognizes as a key role the responsibility to move the flock toward a mature relationship with God.

Active Participation in Your Local Church

Nothing in this book should be read as an indictment the local church is failing at its role as a primary provider of spiritual nourishment to a believer. Absent a strong local church home, the individual Christian will struggle to maintain any of the renewed enthusiasm obtained during a period of personal spiritual retreat. This is not a situation of either-or but rather both. The local church in union with the efforts of the individual believer to deepen his spiritual walk through personal retreat is the appropriate combination for maximum results.

In the ideal situation, the periodic personal retreat is just a supplement to the steady diet of spiritual encouragement received weekly from the local church and its staff. People who take an annual vacation do not stop taking each weekend off from work to renew themselves. Likewise, the individual who takes every weekend off from work should not stop taking at least one annual vacation for a prolonged period of renewal and refreshment. The annual retreat provides something difficult to replicate at the local church—a multiday opportunity for individualized focus on spiritual growth. The local church provides the perfect vehicle

Regaining Your Spiritual Poise

for weekly reinforcement of the call to be sincere followers of Christ. Working in tandem the church and the retreat center can accelerate the spiritual growth of any individual.

Although certainly not universal, many churches are beginning to recognize that they can play a more structured role in the spiritual development of their parishioners. Larger churches are formalizing the role by establishing a position on staff such as director of spiritual formation or director of spiritual growth. Even where a church is of insufficient size to have an individual dedicated to this role, the responsibility to provide spiritual nourishment through focused guidance on spiritual practices is being recognized by many pastors.

When an individual selects his or her church home, there are always multiple considerations. Certainly doctrine is a primary driver of the selection process. Other considerations, such as denomination, proximity to home, size of the congregation, and style of worship also play key roles in the decision process. It is suggested that in addition to all of these criteria, the individual should also consider the church's attitude toward personal spirituality. There are wide variances in practice, and for those who are seeking growth in this area, a church that models and supports such spiritual development would be critical.

Conducting Miniretreats

In Chapter 8 there was a discussion on the appropriate length for individual spiritual retreats. It was suggested that three days could be viewed as a minimum for an organized residential time away in retreat. While that is certainly still advocated, that does not preclude practicing short periods of retreat-like experiences at home or in proximity to home.

These short-term "miniretreats" may only last an hour or two at a time, but they can be particularly effective during a period of stress or challenge in an individual's life. The opportunity to break temporarily from your daily routine and spend some focused time seeking wisdom and guidance through prayer and Scripture reading can prove invaluable.

What is achieved by these miniretreats is something somewhat different from just the daily practice of a quiet time or a period of time reading the Bible. These would be times lasting two to eight hours and would have structures similar to those outlined in chapter ten. One possible way to approach such a time is to carve out small segments of your longer periodic retreat and repeat the exercises contained in a morning or a day. You might also reflect on the activities that you found particularly insightful at your last annual retreat and repeat those exercises.

The key is to find a place in your home or in close proximity where you can have this time alone for purposes of spiritual renewal. If you're the parent of young children, this may require coordinating a babysitter and leaving for a short period of time. You might see if you can have access to a portion of your local church home for the day. You may find that a local park provides sufficient options for contemplative time. You might even consider using your local community library for periods of silent prayer and contemplative reading. Make the time something focused and special. The experience is akin to the idea that even a couple that has been married for decades can benefit by breaking their normal routine by having a "date night" with just the two of them. Remember that one of the things that can dull our spiritual vibrancy is boredom. As in any relationship, breaking old habits can help avoid the complacency that seems to follow whenever we allow ourselves to simply go through the motions.

At first reading this emphasis on variety may seem to contradict the advice regarding discipline. There is a distinct difference. We are commanded to worship God. Waiting until you "feel like it" is not really an option. What is an option is in how you structure your day to demonstrate your love of God through your worship practices. You should provide sufficient structure in your life to ensure that you make communion with God part of your daily routine. As such, you may set aside thirty minutes each morning for this time in relationship. However, some mornings you may take a walk in the woods for a time of prayer. Other mornings you may contemplatively read a short passage of Scripture. The key is to couple consistency with variety in such a way that you maximize your ability to focus during your time with God to draw as close as possible to Him. God is omniscient and omnipresent. As human beings, our skills are considerably less. God is there whenever you are ready to reach out to Him.

Keeping the Spirit of Retreat Alive

One of the primary purposes of spiritual retreat is to deepen your faith and thereby make your relationship with God more meaningful and evident in your daily life. By increasing your understanding of the tenets of your faith and increasing the awareness of God's presence, you are moving to spiritual maturity. As Paul said in Hebrews 5:12–14,

> For though by this time you ought to be teachers, you need someone to teach you again the basic principles of the oracles of God. You need milk, not solid food, for everyone who lives on milk is unskilled in the word of righteousness, since he is a child. But solid food is for the mature, for those who have powers of discernment trained by constant practice to distinguish good from evil.

Someone who makes the spirit of retreat just an annual event to demonstrate his or her own personal piety without having the experience reflected in a changed behavior every other day of the year is like the individual Paul is addressing above. Such people are still drinking milk when they should have moved on long ago to solid food. A diet of solid food prepares the individual believer to distinguish good from evil in their daily lives. This daily walk evidences itself in the discernment the individual Christian exercises in every action he or she takes throughout life.

Becoming a discerning Christian requires that the individual believer learn to love what God loves and hate what God hates. Many Christians find it much easier to be on the hate side of that equation.

They are quick to condemn sin they may see in other's lives. The learning to love what God loves part often tends to be the more difficult part to figure out. That ultimately is the purpose of retreat: to learn how to more deeply love God with every part of our being. That is why exercises advocated in chapter nine were designed to promote loving God with your whole heart, soul, mind, and strength. Following these exercises on a daily basis can reinforce the benefits of retreat throughout the year.

The achievement of personal piety is a result of keeping retreat alive in your life throughout the year, but it is not the primary purpose. The real goal of personal retreat, as was indicated by Evelyn Underhill, is not for our own benefit, but to renew us for the benefit of those around us. It is to renew us to do God's will in God's way during our time in this world. We will then be in a position to hear the words expressed in Matthew 25:23: "Well done good and faithful servant."

Chapter 12: A Short History of Mahseh and Lessons Learned

This chapter will be of a more personal nature and will record a short history of Mahseh Center, the Christian retreat center founded by my wife and myself. I wanted to take this opportunity to record how Mahseh came about, not as any indication of an extraordinary competence on our behalf but as a confirmation of how the Lord can work in wondrous ways in individual lives.

Although Mahseh was opened for guests in April 2008, the story of Mahseh really begins in 1941. My wife Deb's grandfather had moved his family from a farm in the area of the Lake Bruce to South Bend in order to work at the automobile manufacturer Studebaker. He still wanted to stay connected to the area, so he convinced a local farmer who owned the property on the east side of Lake Bruce to sell him approximately two hundred feet of lakefront land. He was able to quickly resell four of the five parcels this represented and made plans to build a small fishing cabin. Before he could start any construction, the attack on Pearl Harbor introduced World War II, and all plans were put on hold.

In 1946 he began construction on a modest six-hundred-square-foot cabin. Due to the scarcity of building materials, the foundation was constructed from fieldstone from local farmland, and the material for the cottage itself was from a dilapidated barn. The cottage did not have any indoor plumbing or running water, but it quickly became the site of many weekend stays by Clarence and Avanga Strong and their family and friends. From the beginning, the 260 acres of placid water held a special appeal to individuals seeking the opportunity to unwind and relax and wet a fishing line.

The south side of Lake Bruce had been a popular site for people looking for an inexpensive location for a vacation or weekend getaway. During the 1920s and 1930s, trains running from Chicago to Cincinnati and points east made daily stops at the local depot. Speculators had built rental cabins, beaches, and even a tall water slide to keep people entertained. Bands performed on summer weekends at a local dance hall. Two small hotels were available for guests. However, in the postwar era, the automobile gave the ordinary family significantly more options on how to spend their vacation time. The trains no longer stopped at Lake Bruce, and the heyday as a tourist destination was over.

People were interested in summer homes, so the character of the lake community changed again. The lake continued to develop on the east side, and eventually the lake was almost entirely ringed with these summer getaways. Northern Indiana has several lakes that were created during the glacier period. Since Lake Bruce was relatively small, boating options were limited, so individuals who built on Lake Bruce were more interested in fishing and peace and quiet. The residents referred to it as a "blue-collar lake" since most of the residents were from factory jobs and the cottages were modest in scale and design. Although a few residents came from Chicago (a two-hour drive away), most were Hoosiers from within an hour or two of the lake.

Clarence suffered a heart attack in early 1956 and died shortly thereafter. With his wife, Avanga, he had five children: Dortha (my wife's mother), Pete, Warren, Clarence Junior, and Phyllis. In 1960 Dortha offered to buy the cottage and pay her mom and siblings for it over a ten-year period. Dortha had married Fred Waidner in 1953, and a little over a year later, my wife, Deborah, was born. Deb has been coming to Lake Bruce literally her whole life. I was introduced to Lake Bruce in the summer of 1973.

Deb and I had begun dating during our freshman year at the University of Indianapolis. I had been born and raised in Indianapolis, so Lake Bruce was an hour closer to my home than driving to Deb's home in Mishawaka, Indiana. My typical routine was to visit at the lake every other weekend during the summer, and I grew to love Lake Bruce as much as the Waidners did.

Deb and I were married on August 21, 1976. For a while we considered having our ceremony on the shores of the lake, but practical concerns over weather and parking led us to a church in her hometown. Even as we both started our careers and purchased our own home, Lake Bruce remained our second home. In 1980 we had the first of our four children, Deidra. She was followed in relatively rapid succession by her three brothers Robert III (Bo) in 1982, Zachary in 1985, and Seth in 1987. Dortha had remodeled the cabin in 1973 to add a bathroom and expand the living room at the cabin, but with our growing family, things were beginning to become a little crowded.

Deb and I began to consider whether or not we should look for another home on the lake. In the spring of 1998, the neighbors adjacent to the north of the cottage casually mentioned that they were considering retiring permanently to Florida and would be putting their house on the market. Before they could say anything else Deb shouted, "We'll buy it!" The neighbor then asked if we were interested in knowing the purchase price. Our bargaining position was severely weakened, but a fair price was then mentioned. In August of 1998 we closed on what we began to call "the red cottage" because of its stained red siding. What made this piece of property particularly appealing is that it was actually composed of three of the normal lots. Deb's parents' cottage (which they had named Dunrovin) sat on a forty-foot-wide lot. The red cottage had a 120-foot lot, which provided a lot of outdoor space for our children to run around in.

Now that we had a cottage of our own, we felt more comfortable inviting friends and family to share the space and the rest and renewal Lake Bruce provided. Sometime during this period, Deb and I began to discuss the thought of accumulating other property for the express purpose of offering it to others for spiritual retreat. We ourselves had felt renewed by some of our personal experiences at Christian camps and retreat centers and knew the power of time away for renewal. At this point, it was no more than a "wouldn't it be nice if ..." moment with no specific plans. We had a young and growing family to occupy our time, so we were very open to letting God reveal His plan for us as His timing dictated.

As a couple of years more passed, we began to think about the property to the north of the red cottage as a parcel worth acquiring. Both Dunrovin and the red cottage were functional but not particularly attractive architecturally. They had seven-foot ceilings and were more or less square floor plans. They were finished in sheet paneling and artificial ceilings. The adjacent parcel had been constructed in 1969 and was of a classic A-frame construction. The interior was comprised of cedar one-by-five boards that had aged into a beautiful honey-brown color. The cathedral ceilings gave a feeling of spaciousness that belied the small square footage. It needed significant updating, but it was worth the effort to bring it up to current standards.

On a whim, I wrote a letter asking the owners if they would consider selling it. We had noted they had only been using it two or three times a summer for the last few years. To our joy, they were willing to sell, and in April 2002 we closed on the property and began the renovation. We moved our family to the A-frame, and the red cottage became available for family and friends to use free of charge for their space.

Shortly after moving into the A-frame, one problem became obvious. Immediately next to the A-frame there was a small group of cabins available under the name of Lake Bruce Resorts. When constructed in the 1950s, they were likely very attractive, but fifty years of wear and tear with limited maintenance had taken its toll. In their current condition, the owner was willing to rent them to about anyone at a very inexpensive price. On our first night there a motorcycle gang had rented the resort for a beer and fishing weekend. Needless to say, having parties going on late into the night within a few feet of our property diminished some of our enthusiasm for our new home.

The next morning I approached the owner and inquired what his plans were for the property. I had heard it was for sale but did not have any idea of the asking price. He informed me he was going through a divorce and his soon-to-be-ex-wife was very anxious for her half of the sales proceeds. Having nothing to lose I made him a rather unusual offer. I told him I was only interested in the property and not the cabins or their contents. I offered him two-thirds of his asking price but also told him he could auction off all of the furniture and equipment. Furthermore, the cabins were all constructed from kits with no internal framing. They could be disassembled and sold as well. We had a deal!

At this point in time, Deb and I thought the Lord was beginning to crystalize our vision for a retreat center. With this additional space, we could envision constructing another structure or maybe a series of cabins for guests. It would likely be years in the future since we were only in our late forties, but at least we had the property. At the same time, God was constructing an even better plan.

In 1989, just to the south of Dunrovin, a couple named Norm and Barb Steigely had purchased the cabin next door. Over the next few years, just as we had purchased properties to the north of Dunrovin, Norm began to purchase properties to the south. In fact, between the two of us, we now controlled all of the properties that Clarence, Deb's grandfather, had originally purchased over sixty years earlier and then some. In the spring of 1994, Norm surprised us and everyone else on the lake by tearing down three of the cottages he had purchased and began construction of an enormous house that was over eight thousand square feet under roof.

I had mentioned earlier that Lake Bruce was a "blue-collar lake." This house was probably ten times the size of the average cottage on the lake. Norm had sold his business earlier that year and felt that Lake Bruce was going to be his and Barb's home for the rest of their lives, so he wanted to build his "dream home."

We watched over the next eighteen months as the house was constructed. The quality and care that Norm put into the house were incredible. If standard building code would require twelve-inch foundation walls, Norm built twenty-four-inch walls. If two-by-sixes on eighteen-inch center were the standard floor choice, the new home would be built with two-by-twelve's on twelve-inch center. The woodwork and hardwood floors were the finest that could be found. It was not only a large home, but also one that was constructed to last for decades. At the time, Deb and I could not figure out why Norm was building such a house. We had no complaints, because we figured it could only add to the value of our neighboring property. But within a ten-year period, the purpose of the property became much clearer in both our minds and those of Norm and Barb.

Due to a change in financial circumstances that occurred in the late 1990s, Norm and Barb decided that the home they had constructed was no longer viable to own and maintain. Finally, in 2002, they put the home on the market. As with any real estate, location is critical to value. As mentioned above, the house was out of character with the remainder of the properties on the lake. Despite repeatedly lowering the purchase price, as the years rolled forward, the house remained unsold. Norm had approached my wife and me several times about purchasing the home for our own personal use. Although a beautiful home, it was too large and did not suit our personal taste. By the summer of 2005, the Steigelys were to the point where they were on the brink of allowing the home to fall into foreclosure.

One afternoon Deb and I discussed that maybe God was opening up the possibility of the home becoming our base for the retreat center we had been discussing. From a practical perspective, it did not make much sense. The biggest issue was that between what the home was worth and what we thought we could raise to purchase it there seemed to be too far a gap. Besides, the timing did not seem right. I was still several years from retirement, and we would be practically absentee owners for some period of time.

One other very practical consideration existed. All the cottages on the lake were on a septic system. As large as the Steigley's home was, it was technically limited to three bedrooms. Norm had established a conservation district around the lake as the legal entity to build a sewer. However, if he left, there really was no one else available to spend the hours needed to make the sewer systems a reality.

Still, God seemed to be saying, "Trust Me!" We had shared our feeling of a call to open the retreat center with several friends. We asked them to be praying for us. We contacted a handful of them that weekend and asked them to pray specifically for wisdom and guidance. Over the next few days a plan began to formulate. We made Norm and Barb the following offer. We would create a corporate charitable entity to purchase the home. The purchase would be contingent upon the Steigelys continuing to live in the home until the sewers were near or at completion. We also could only offer a purchase price that approximated 40 percent of the original construction cost. We felt that if the Steigelys accepted this offer, it would be a sign that God wanted us to move forward.

The next day, in November 2005, we presented the offer to Norm and Barb. They asked for a couple of days to think about it but in fact walked back over to our summer home within the hour. God had moved their hearts, and they had a vision for the work. To quote Norm, "We might be able to get more money by holding out, but we would rather see you guys get it and use the house to honor the Lord."

I am sure you have had the experience where you hoped and prayed for something, but once received, the reality of the challenge of what you asked for stares you in the face. You move from exaltation to concern to abject fear in relatively quick order. Despite this normal reaction, the peace of God quickly descended on us. After all, if He can be for us, who can be against us?

The purchase transaction closed in January 2006. At that point in time we only needed to raise approximately half of the purchase price of the home, which represented the outstanding mortgage on the property. The remainder would be due when the sewers were complete and Norm and Barb vacated the home. That date was not to occur for another twenty-seven months.

During this gap period, there was still a lot of preparatory work to be done. Norm enlisted me to help with the financial analysis of the feasibility of the sewer project. Later, we needed to collect signatures from at least 51 percent of the residents of the lake endorsing the sewer project. This was followed by grant applications and then the actual sewer construction.

Inside Mahseh itself, we began construction to move the home from a purely personal residence to a facility that could house up to twenty people. This required moving interior walls and creating four additional bedrooms. Knowing that we wanted the facility to be a study and retreat center, we needed to build out library space and improve the technology infrastructure. We also needed to name the place so that we could begin to build a website and prepare some limited public education material about the center.

I have been an avid reader and follower of Francis and Edith Schaeffer and the L'Abri movement for decades. I have no doubt that reading the story of L'Abri had a significant impact on our desire to create a retreat and study center. Although our ministry was going to have a different focus, the concept of place evident in the Schaeffers' work was key. I knew that *L'Abri* in French meant "the shelter." I asked our son Zach, who was studying Hebrew at Taylor University at the time, if he could give me some words in Hebrew that conveyed the similar concept of shelter or retreat. Zach suggested Anglicizing the Hebrew word for *refuge,* and the word and ministry of Mahseh was born.

The sewers for Lake Bruce were completed in the spring of 2008, the final piece of the transaction was complete, and Norm and Barb moved to another home on the lake. We were grateful that they were going to stay around to see that their efforts in constructing the home would be blessed by God. Their departure also meant that God needed to provide us with someone to help us manage the facility and take care of the many details that would need attention.

Although I would have desired to retire from my work at Ernst & Young at that time, the economics did not appear to permit it. Besides, being in a position where I needed to work to support my family, I was also five years away from fully accruing my pension. As a senior partner with EY, I was at the prime of my earnings years. I realized that if I really wanted to keep Mahseh on sound financial footing and allow for expansion of the ministry, my best option was to continue in my "tent making" and find someone to be the director of Mahseh.

Having the benefit of hindsight, I continue to be amazed at God's providence in providing the right staff at the right time in our ministry. As we launched the ministry of Mahseh, God brought Mark Eckel into my life.

Mark had taught at Moody Bible Institute in Chicago for a number of years. He had moved to Indianapolis about a year before we met to head up a program to introduce a new curriculum at a local private Christian high school. Shortly after his arrival, the headmaster that had hired Mark was dismissed, and Mark was going to find a new position at the end of the school year. We met, appropriately enough, at the men's retreat from my home church in November 2006. He explained his situation and that he was going to be looking for part-time employment as he worked to complete his doctoral thesis. In what appeared to be a match made in heaven, Mark came on board as our first director of Mahseh. We were now set to open our doors.

Our first group arrived on the first weekend in May of 2008. Appropriately enough, it was Deb and my long-time pastor and his wife, Tom and Judy Streeter, who brought the first group to Mahseh. They were followed by other groups from our church and other individuals and groups in the area who had heard about what we were trying to do.

As a ministry, we had decided not to do any true advertising or marketing. We would be available on the web should someone look for a Northern Indiana retreat center, but we would be open to whom the Lord would bring to our doorsteps. The same would be true for our finances. We would suggest to people what they might pay to cover some of our variable costs for their stay, but no one would be refused who could not pay. In addition, these suggested amounts would only approximate one-third of the costs of similar lodging at a bed-and-breakfast or hotel. We wanted to keep Mahseh accessible to everyone and rely on God to provide the remaining income for construction and operations. Like in most faith ministries, money has been tight on occasion, but the Lord has been very faithful to provide resources when most needed.

The growth in occupancy has been geometric over the initial five years. Word of mouth has been a very effective tool in letting people know of our ministry. A large percentage of the groups and individuals who have attended once now repeat their visits at least annually.

Over the initial three years, the Lord provided a patchwork of hardworking individuals to help with the ministry. Mark concentrated on the creation of the extensive library collection and also authored and conducted several seminars and original works. Richard Green and his son Dale provided care to the extensive grounds and gardens of the home. Michael Hiatt and his construction crew handled repairs and new construction and remodeling work on the premises. Max Weiss, an intern, capably indexed the library and helped out wherever possible. We had found an outstanding lady to clean the house. Sharon Glasson keeps Mahseh so incredibly neat it literally looks better than on the day we moved in, despite thousands of overnight stays since we opened. She has been a blessing to us and everyone who has visited Mahseh.

Deb and I made the drive from Zionsville to Lake Bruce every weekend and handled the scheduling and finances remotely. Although this amalgamation of individuals did a remarkable job, it became apparent we needed a more permanent full-time solution to bridge us to my anticipated retirement in the summer of 2012.

In the fall of 2010, God provided the perfect answer to Mahseh's need in the form of my brother and sister-in-law Ron and Alison Wingerter. Ron is a mechanical engineer by training and spent all of his career as a plant engineer at various large manufacturing facilities. Alison is a nurse who spent most of her time homeschooling their four daughters. Mark Eckel had completed his doctorate and was ready to assume a full-time position at an Indianapolis-based Bible college as an academic dean. Ron and Alison had followed the growth of Mahseh, and upon Mark's departure they approached us about working full-time at Mahseh.

The blessing they have been to Mahseh cannot be overstated. The skill sets Ron and Alison bring to the ministry are entirely complementary to those of Deb and me. My strengths are in the financial and legal area as well as long-term visioning and teaching. Deb has administrative skills that are outstanding and coordinates all of the details regarding scheduling. Ron keeps the grounds immaculate and the facility in tip-top shape. Alison focuses on the gardens and keeping the interior warm and hospitable. We all work in ministering to our many guests. To have a brother and sister-in-law in fact who are also a brother and sister in the Lord and partners in ministry has been a tremendous blessing that I thank the Lord for on a daily basis. Even with just three years to look back upon, it is very evident to me that Mahseh would not be the wonderful place it has become without Ron and Alison's efforts.

I would be remiss if I didn't spend a short time thanking my wife Deb for her constant support and affirmation of the ministry of Mahseh. Dedications are usually reserved for the front of the book, but the vision of Mahseh has been truly a collaboration between both of us. Her love of the Lord and desire to serve Him has kept me focused on this ministry when I could have easily drifted away, consumed by any number of other "good ideas." Visionaries often have this problem of practical focus, and she has been my rock of consistency. While I tend to think of the "big picture," she "sweats the details." There is no question that she is the helpmate God picked out for me when He set our paths on the vision of this ministry years ago.

Lessons Learned

As I write this book, Mahseh has been in full-time operation for a little over five years. In one sense this is a very new ministry. In another, this is a ministry that has been going on in some form of fashion for two millennia. I challenged myself to write this book upon my retirement to solidify a vision for where Mahseh fits within God's plan for me as an individual and the people He brings to our door. Although many of the thoughts expressed in this book were formulated years ago from a variety of experiences, the activity around establishing and running Mahseh has made them concrete enough to make a record of. The following are among the most poignant of these lessons.

(1) Satan loves to distract us, and in our fallen state we are very prone to being distracted. He doesn't need to turn us into heretics to rob us of the joy of our salvation. The daily activities of life lead us to lose focus on what is important by distracting us with what appears urgent.

(2) When we feel like God is distant, it is because we have moved away from Him—not Him from us. We have not nurtured the most critical relationship we will ever have. When we lead our lives like "practical atheists," it should not be a surprise to us that we don't feel His presence. It is not that God does not care for each and every one of us. He created us and loves us with a love beyond compare. But we would not be true to our nature of being made in His image if we didn't have the free will to act on our own—even when those actions separate us from Him.

(3) We are not alone in struggling with this life of wandering from His presence. People from all previous generations have struggled with the same issue. Coming to a saving knowledge of the grace of God as represented by Christ on the cross is only the first step in His daily desire to see us grow in our spiritual maturity. If we are not so myopic to believe that this generation has all the answers, we can access a wealth of information on how other believers before us have structured their lives to draw closer to God.

(4) Although others over the years have found that totally extracting themselves from the day-to-day activities of this world by adopting a monastic lifestyle is the answer to Christian maturity, it is not the answer for the vast majority of Christians. We are called to be salt and light in the world. However, to withdraw on a temporary basis for even a few days to refocus and rededicate ourselves to living the victorious Christian life can help immeasurably in the constant battle to regain our spiritual poise.

(5) These times away are invaluable, so they cannot be spent in an unstructured way. The practice of spiritual disciplines is key to maximizing what God has planned for us during these times. The primary focus of this retreat time is to make God's presence so real that as you depart you are confident in the basis of your faith and how it should be reflected in your daily walk.

(6) You cannot make this heightened state of awareness in God's presence a once-a-year exercise. The real goal is to use the time of retreat to refocus and grow in your understanding of God and then to carry that forward to your daily life. This may require you to reground yourself in some of the experiences of your retreat time. The biggest key to success is to make time in your daily routine to spend with God. That sounds a lot simpler than it is in reality. Only by doing it day after day until it becomes an ingrained habit will you likely succeed.

(7) The time of retreat is not to be just for our benefit but for the benefit of the world around us. With renewed focus and corrected priorities, we are better equipped to help those around us who are less fortunate. We cannot earn our way into heaven with our actions, but our actions send a clear message to the unbelieving world that our faith has made a difference in how we live our lives.

I pray that you gain a small measure of the benefit of reading this book that I did in writing it. Although I have studied at Bible school and seminary, I am not a theologian or a cleric. I spent the last forty years of my life as a businessman and family man. I write from knowing the real struggles of conducting ourselves as Christian men and women in a world that every day finds the label of *Christian* less and less relevant. I know the realities of having to struggle to maintain your spiritual poise. My sincere hope is that in some small measure this book and more importantly the practices outlined in it will help you in regaining your spiritual poise.

Regaining Your Spiritual Poise

Addendum A
Christian Classics Reading List

On several occasions in the book, it is recommended that you spend a portion of your retreat time reading one of the "Christian classics." While a few are named within the book itself, the following list of titles was accumulated to provide additional guidance. The term "Christian classic" is a term of art versus science. In general, these are books that have been in publication for years (or some cases centuries) and have been recognized as providing unique insights into the human soul and its relationship with God. The list certainly is not exhaustive, and there are numerous other books that could be added to this list. This list stopped at one hundred. The books suggested are not all of a purely spiritual nature. Some are historical or theological in focus. Others are allegorical or apologetic. However, time spent reading any of them is well spent. A book's presence on the list should not be taken as an endorsement for everything contained within it. However, the thoughts expressed are by and large orthodox and in conformity with traditional Christian doctrine. They are presented in no particular order other than alphabetically by title.

Title	Author
A Closer Walk	Catherine Marshall
A Mirror for Simple Souls	Marguerite Porete
A Serious Call to a Devout and Holy Life	William Law
A Testament of Devotion	Thomas R. Kelly
A Treatise Concerning Religious Affections	Jonathan Edwards
Basic Christianity	John Stott
Bondage of the Will	Martin Luther
Calling	Oz Guinness
City of God	Saint Augustine of Hippo
Confessions	Saint Augustine of Hippo
Creation in Christ	George McDonald
Dark Night of the Soul	Saint John of the Cross
Desiring God	John Piper
Diary and Life of Andrew Bonar	Marjory Bonar
Echoes from Eden	A. W. Tozer
Evidence That Demands a Verdict	Josh McDowell
Experiencing the Depths of Jesus Christ	Jeanne Guyon
Fox's Book of Martyrs	John Fox
Fundamentalism and American Culture	George M. Marsden
Growing in Christ	J. I. Packer
Habits of the Heart	Robert Bellah, et al.

Holiness	John Charles Ryle
How Should We Then Live?	Francis Schaeffer
How the Irish Saved Civilization	Thomas Cahill
How to Pray	Jean-Nicholas Gross
Institutes of Christian Religion	John Calvin
Introduction to the Devout Life	Francis de Sales
Knowing God	J. I. Packer
Know Why You Believe	Paul E. Little
Life Together	Dietrich Bonhoeffer
Mere Christianity	C. S. Lewis
Moral Man and Immoral Society	Reinhold Niebuhr
Mysticism	Evelyn Underhill
My Utmost for His Highest	Oswald Chambers
Notes on the Miracles of the Lord	Richard Trench
On Free Choice of the Will	Saint Augustine of Hippo
On the Incarnation	Saint Athanasius
On Prayer	E. M. Bounds
Orthodoxy	G. K. Chesterton
Paradise Lost	John Milton
Parochial and Plain Sermons	John Henry Newman
Paul Apostle of the Heart Set Free	F. F. Bruce
Pensées	Blaise Pascal

Pilgrim's Progress	John Bunyon
Pilgrim at Tinker Creek	Annie Dillard
Prayer and Conversations with God	Rosalind Rinker
Prayer and Worship	Douglas V. Steere
Private Devotions of Lancelot Adams	Lancelot Adams
Redeeming Love	Francine Rivers
Prayer	Richard Foster
Revelations of Divine Love	Julian of Norwich
Self-Abandonment to Divine Providence	Jean Pierre de Caussade
Simply Jesus	N. T. Wright
Sit Walk Stand	Watchman Nee
Sun Dancing	Geoffrey Moorhouse
The Adventure of Living	Paul Tournier
The Cloud of Unknowing	Anonymous
The Cost of Discipleship	Dietrich Bonhoeffer
The Cross of Christ	John Stott
The Dialogue	Catherine of Siena
The Distinguishing Marks of a Work of the Spirit of God	Jonathan Edwards
The Divine Comedy	Dante Aleghieri
The Divine Conspiracy	Dallas Willard
The Divine Milieu	Pierre Tielhard de Chardin

The Everlasting Man	G. K. Chesteron
The Four Cardinal Virtues	Josef Pieper
The Four Loves	C. S. Lewis
The Glory of Christ	John Owen
The God Who Is There	Francis Schaeffer
The Gospel in a Pluralist Society	Leslie Newbigin
The Great Divorce	C. S. Lewis
The Healing Light	Agnes Sanford
The Idea of the Holy	Rudolf Otto
The Imitation of Christ	Thomas a Kempis
The Interior Castle	Teresa of Avila
The Jesus I Never Knew	Philip Yancey
The Journal of George Fox	George Fox
The Journal of John Woolman	John Woolman
The Knowledge of God	A. W. Tozer
The Life of God in the Soul of Man	Henry Scrougal
The Living Christ and the Four Gospels	R. W. Dale
The Long Loneliness	Dorothy Day
The Love of God	Bernard of Clairvaux
The Meaning of Persons	Paul Tournier
The Mind of the Maker	Dorothy L. Sayers
The Normal Christian Life	Watchman Nee

Endnotes

Every reasonable effort has been made to determine copyright holders of excerpted materials. If any copyrighted materials have been inadvertently used without proper credit being given in one form or another, please notify Rob Wingerter (9902 East 200 South, Zionsville, IN 46077) in writing so that future editions may be corrected accordingly.

1. Evelyn Underhill, *The Fruits of the Spirit* (Harrisburg: Morehouse Publishing, 1982), 5.

2. Romans 1:21,2:5

3. Francis A. Schaeffer, *Escape from Reason*. London: Intervarsity Press, 1968).

4. Francis A. Schaeffer, *The God Who Is There* (Westmont: Intervarsity Press, 1968).

5. Georg Wilhelm Friedrich Hegel (1770–1831) was a German philosopher known for his concept of Absolute Idealism.

6. Proverbs 30:8–9.

7. Exodus 2–3.

8. Neil Postman, *Amusing Ourselves to Death* (New York: Penguin Books, 1985).

9. http://www:statisticbrain.com/reading-statistics

10. Mathew 5:13

11. 2 Timothy 2:3–4

12. 1 Timothy 1:12

13. "Put on the whole armor of God that you may be able to stand against the schemes of the devil."

14. Sojourners Bible verse

15. Dorothy Bass, *Practicing Our Faith* (Hoboken: Josey Bass Publishing, 2009).

16. Bass, *Practicing Our Faith*, xxiii.

17. Charles Schultz, *Peanuts Comic Strip* (United Features Syndicate, September 4, 1975).

18. Daniel G. Reid, ed., *Dictionary of Christianity in America* (IVP Press, 1990), 949.

19. Reid, *Dictionary of Christianity in America*, 461

20. Developed in the 1830s in England, this interpretation of the Bible divides all time into seven different stages of God's revelation. According to this theory, at the end of each stage God punishes humanity for having been found wanting during a period of testing. Under this view the world is on the verge of the last stage, which is to end with a "last battle" to be followed the thousand-year reign of Christ on earth.

21. http://www.wheaton.edu/ISAE/Defining-Evangelicalism/Defining-the-Term

22. George Marsden, *Reforming Fundamentalism* (Grand Rapids: Wm. B. Eerdmans Publishing, 1995), 48.

23. Randall Herbert Balmer, *Encyclopedia of Evangelicalism First Edition* (Louisville: Westminster John Knox Press, 2002).

24. 1 Samuel 13:14

25. Judges 13–16

26. James 2:26

27. Max Weber, *The Protestant Work Ethic and the Spirit of Capitalism.* Blacksburg: Wilder Publishing, 1905).

28. Daniel S. Reid and Robert D. Linder, *Dictionary of Christianity in America* (2004), 951.

29. Mark 12:30

30. *General Instructions of the Roman Missal* (Washington: United States Conference of Catholic Bishops, 2011).

31. *General Instructions of the Roman Missal*, paragraph 78.

32. *General Instructions of the Roman Missal,* paragraph 160.

33. Bishop Kolistas Ware, *The Orthodox Church* (London: Penguin Books, 1997), 280.

34. Ware, *The Orthodox Church*, 242.

35. Ware, *The Orthodox Church*, 268.

36. Ware, *The Orthodox Church*, 204.

37. Ware, *The Orthodox Church*, 300.

38. Ware, *The Orthodox Church*, 30–32.

39. Ephesians 2:8

40. Mathew 28:19

41. Acts 2

42. Justo L. Gonzalez, *The Story of Christianity, Volume I* (New York: HarperCollins Publishers, 1984), 31.

43. Gonzalez, *The Story of Christianity, Volume I*, 34.

44. Gonzalez, *The Story of Christianity, Volume I*, 107.

45. Gonzalez, *The Story of Christianity, Volume I*, 136.

46. Gonzalez, *The Story of Christianity, Volume I*, 137.

47. Gonzalez, *The Story of Christianity, Volume I*, 138.

48. Marilyn Dunn, *The Emergence of Monasticism*, (Oxford: Blackwell Publishing, 2003), 2

49. E. C. Butler, "St. Anthony," in *The Catholic Encyclopedia* (New York: Robert Appleton Company, 1907).

50. Dunn, *The Emergence of Monasticism*, 4.

51. Gonzalez, *The Story of Christianity, Volume I*, 142.

52. Gonzalez, *The Story of Christianity, Volume I*, 143.

53. Gonzalez, *The Story of Christianity, Volume I*, 144.

54. Gonzalez, *The Story of Christianity, Volume I*, 146.

55. Gonzalez, *The Story of Christianity, Volume I*, 146.

56. *The Life of Saint Martin*

57. Gonzalez, *The Story of Christianity, Volume I*, 239.

58. *The Rule of Saint Benedict*

59. Gonzalez, *The Story of Christianity, Volume I*, 239.

60. Dorothy C. Bass, ed., *Practicing our Faith, Second Edition,* (San Francisco: John Wiley & Sons, 2010), 49

61. Dunn, *The Emergence of* Monasticism, 61.

62. Dunn, *The Emergence of* Monasticism, 61.

63. Dunn, *The Emergence of* Monasticism, 64.

64. Dunn, *The Emergence of* Monasticism, 67.

65. Dunn, *The Emergence of* Monasticism, 68.

66. Bass, ed., *Practicing our Faith*, 50

67. Bass, ed., *Practicing our Faith*, 64

68. For a fascinating account of this aspect of the Monastic movement, see Thomas Cahill's *How the Irish Saved Civilization.*

69. Gonzalez, *The Story of Christianity, Volume I*, 241

70. Gonzalez, *The Story of Christianity, Volume I*, 216

71. C. H. Lawrence, *Medieval Monasticism*, (Pearson Education Limited, 1984), 41.

72. Lawrence, *Medieval Monasticism*, 42.

73. Lawrence, *Medieval Monasticism*, 44.

74. Lawrence, *Medieval Monasticism*, 46.

75. Lawrence, *Medieval Monasticism*, 51.

76. Galatians 3:28

77. Dunn, *The Emergence of* Monasticism, chapter 3.

78. W. K. L. Clarke, trans., *St. Gregory: The Life of St. Macrina* (London, 1916), 23.

79. Dunn, *The Emergence of* Monasticism, 45.

80. Lawrence, *Medieval Monasticism*, 109–110.

81. Lawrence, *Medieval Monasticism*, 84–85.

82. Lawrence, *Medieval Monasticism*, chapter 6.

83. Lawrence, *Medieval Monasticism*, 173–175.

84. C. J. Holdsworth, Studies of Church History 10, (London: Baker Press, 1955).

85. Gonzalez, *The Story of Christianity, Volume I*, 282.

86. Lawrence, *Medieval Monasticism*, 238.

87. Lawrence, *Medieval Monasticism*, 207–209.

88. Lawrence, *Medieval Monasticism*, 209–212

89. Lawrence, *Medieval Monasticism*, 238.

90. Lawrence, *Medieval Monasticism*, 238.

91. *The Franciscan Cypberspot,* website maintained by the Franciscans of Malta, established 1996.

92. Justo L. Gonzalez, *The Story of Christianity Volume II,* (San Francisco: Harpers, 1985), 114–115

93. Nancy Pearcey, *Total Truth* (Wheaton: Crossway Books, 2004), 81

94. Gordon Mursell, ed., *The Story of Christian Spirituality* (Minneapolis: Fortress Press, 2001), 9.

95. 2 Timothy 3:16

96. Richard J. Foster, ed., *25 Books Every Christian Should Read* (New York: Harper One Press, 2011), 93.

97. Foster, ed., *25 Books Every Christian Should Read*, 93.

98. Nicholas Watson and Jacqueline Jenkins, eds., *The Writings of Julian of Norwich* (Brepols, 2006).

99. F. Beer, *Women and Mystical Experiences in the Middle Ages* (Boydell Press, 1992), 143–144.

100. Julian of Norwich, forward by Thomas Merton, *Revelations of Divine Love* (Anthony Clarke Publishing, 1973).

101. Mursell, ed., *The Story of Christian Spirituality*, 122.

102. Foster, ed., *25 Books Every Christian Should Read*, 108.

103. Mursell, ed., *The Story of Christian Spirituality*, 122.

104. Foster, ed., *25 Books Every Christian Should Read*, 108.

105. Mursell, ed., *The Story of Christian Spirituality*, 231.

106. Brother Lawrence, E. Blaiklock, trans., *The Practice of the Presence of God* (London: Hodder & Stoughon, 1982), 85.

107. Foster, ed., *25 Books Every Christian Should Read*, 204.

108. I Thessalonians 5:17

109. http://www.theosophytrust.org/tlodocs/articlesTeacher.php?d=WilliamLaw.htm&p=137

110. ibid

111. William Law, John Meister, ed., *A Serious Call to a Devout and Holy Life,* (Philadelphia: The Westminster Press, 1955).

112. Richard J. Foster and James Bryan Smith, eds., *Devotional Classics,* (San Francisco: Harper Publishing, 1993), 112

113. Charles Williams, ed., *The Letters of Evelyn Underhill* (Longman Green Press), 122.

114. E. M. Bounds, *Power Through Prayer* (Chicago: Moody Press, n.d.), 23.

115. Bounds, *Power Through Prayer*, 38.

116. James Strong, Strong's Concordance of the Bible (Nashville: Thomas Nelson Publishers, 1990), 834–835.

117. Nathan Bailey, *A Universal Etymological English Dictionary* (London Press, 1773).

118. George Lane, *Christian Spirituality: A Historical Sketch,* ISBN 0-8294-2081-9, 20.

119. Richard Foster, *Celebration of Discipline* (New York) Harper & Row, 1978, pages 55-56.

120. Lynne M. Baab, *Fasting, A Spiritual Freedom Beyond Our Appetites* (Downers Grove: Intervarsity Press, 2006), 16.

121. Foster, *Celebration of Discipline,* 86.

122. Dallas Willard, *Spirit of the Disciplines* (Harper Collins Press, 1990), 161.

123. Exodus 3:2

124. Donald G. Bloesch, *Spirituality Old & New* (Downers Grove: IVP Academic, 2007), 35–43.

125. Bloesch, *Spirituality Old & New,* 38.

126. Bloesch, *Spirituality Old & New,* 40.

127. Jonathan R. Wilson, *Living Faithfully in a Fragmented World* (Harrisburg: Trinity Press International, 1998).

128. Wilson, *Living Faithfully in a Fragmented World,* 72–75.

129. Rutba House, *School(s) for Conversion: 12 Marks of a New Monasticism* (2005), xii–xiii.

130. Philip Zaleski, *The Recollected Heart* (Notre Dame: Ave Maria Press, 1995), 55.

131. Robert W. Gleason, *Introduction to The Spiritual Exercises of Saint Ignatius* (New York: Doubleday Press, 1964), 11–12.

132. Gleason, *Introduction to The Spiritual Exercises of Saint Ignatius*, 14–15.

133. Nevill Drury, *The New Age: Searching for the Spiritual Self* (London: Thomas and Henderson, 2004), 14.

134. Drury, *The New Age: Searching for the Spiritual Self*, 8.

135. Robert W. Gleason, *Introduction to The Spiritual Exercises of Saint Ignatius* (New York: Image Books, 1964), 22.

136. Gleason, *Introduction to The Spiritual Exercises of Saint Ignatius*, 22.

137. Gleason, *Introduction to The Spiritual Exercises of Saint Ignatius*, 37.

138. Gleason, *Introduction to The Spiritual Exercises of Saint Ignatius*, 47–128.

139. Lonni Pratt and Daniel Homan, *Benedict's Way* (Chicago: Loyola Press, 2000).

140. John 3:16

141. Aristotle, *On The Soul,* 412b5.

142. Thomas Aquinas, *Summa Theologeia,* Question 75.

143. Clive Staple Lewis, *Letters to Malcolm: Chiefly on Prayer* (New York: Harcourt Brace Jovanovich, 1964) 114–115.

144. Alexis de Tocqueville, *Democracy in America* (London: Penguin Press, trans. 2003).

Made in the USA
Lexington, KY
07 March 2014